Shibari for]

A Step by Step Guide, with Detailed Pictures for Beginners to Master The Old Japanese Rope Bonding.

Jennifer Ichika

© **Copyrights 2022 – all rights reserved.**

The contents of this book may not be reproduced, duplicated, or transmitted without direct written permission from the author or publisher.

No blame or legal responsibility will be held against the publisher or author for any damages, reparations, or monetary loss due to the information contained in this book. Whether directly or indirectly.

Disclaimer notice:

Please note that the information within this document is for educational and entertainment purposes only. All efforts have been made to present reliable and complete information, and no warranties are implied or declared.

The trademarks used are without any consent, and the publication of the trademark is without permission or backing by the owner. All trademarks and brands within this book are for clarifying purposes only and are owned by the owners, not affiliated with this document.

Table of Content

CHAPTER ONE 1
  INTRODUCTION TO SHIBARI 1
    What is Shibari? 1

CHAPTER TWO 9
  OVERVIEW OF ROPE TYPES 9
    Rope Selection & Care 9
    A Guide to Selection 10
    Natural-Fiber Rope 13
    Synthetic Rope 15
    HEMP 17
    Cotton 18
    Rope Ends 21
    Size 23
    Typical Number of Ropes 25
    Rope & Style 25

CHAPTER THREE 28
  BASIC KNOTS 28
    Bight Vs. Open Loop 30
    Slipped knot 30
    Lark's Head 34
    Square Knot 35
    Prusik Head Knot 35
    Cross Hitch Friction 37
    Double Coin Knot 37
    Inline Double Coin Knot 38
    Using The Bight As A Pulley 41
    Double-Column Shibari Tie 43

CHAPTER FOUR 47
  CHEST HARNESS 47

iii

Extending Rope	*56*
CHAPTER FIVE	**59**
HOW TO TIE ROPE ARMBINDER	59
How To Create The Chest Harness	*90*
CHAPTER SIX	**109**
THE BENEFITS	109

Introduction

Rope bondage is comforting to me because of its deliberate repetition and exact design. As a rope top, no matter what else is going on in my life, I have to be present to focus on the ties, the bottom I'm tying up, and the tone of the encounter. I get off on the bottom both giving up control and having fun.

For a bottom, being restrained can also feel very calming. A lot of bottoms feel relaxed and blissed out while in rope. One told me: "I like giving over control to the top, letting them do whatever they want to me and feeling their power as they tie. I also really like the sensation; the pain and restriction feel exquisite." Another said: "As someone who gets off on giving up power/control, I really enjoy the psychological sensation of being restrained, as well as the challenge of persevering through discomfort. That feeling of someone else/the rope controlling how my body is able to move is freeing to me; I don't have to make decisions, I don't have to be in control, but in a safe context. It's soothing, and makes me feel focused and light and able to be very present."

Playing with rope bondage is usually an emotionally intimate space to share. It can be rough and sexual, soft and non-sexual, or anywhere in between.

Chapter One

Introduction to Shibari

What is Shibari?

Shibari (also often referred to as kinbaku) is a form of Japanese rope bondage It differs from Western rope bondage in a few areas, including the use of non-stretchy natural fiber rope, such as hemp or jute, rather than softer cotton, silk, or polyester rope, the emphasis on friction and wrapping rather than knots, and the use of rope that has been doubled over in the middle., a point called the bight, and works down toward the ends; and it has a deep focus on the aesthetic of the ties.

Shibari uses building blocks and repeated patterns that fit together to create ties. Once you learn these blocks and patterns and some basic safety, you can often figure out how to repeat a tie you see elsewhere.

(You'll learn several of these building blocks in the rest of this series.)

Shibari is derived from Hojojutsu, a martial art used in the Edo period (1600 to the mid-1800s) by the Samurai to arrest and restrain prisoners with rope. Often prisoners were publicly shamed by being displayed tied in ropes, which usually conveyed their class and crime, before execution or imprisonment. Hojojutsu died away at the end of the Edo period when the shogunates were overthrown.

People in Japan started to use the Hojojutsu ties for BDSM, and to play with the physical restraint and emotional shame of being tied. This art of tight and often painful sexual or sensual tying became known as shibari (decorative tying) or kinbaku (tight binding).

More recently, shibari has started to become popular in BDSM communities worldwide. While those who are not Japanese won't be able to fully understand or experience the shame aspect of being tied, the complexity, efficiency and attractiveness of the ties themselves have earned appreciation for this style of rope bondage. Some of the most popular Japanese performers and rope tops even travel worldwide to perform on stage or to teach classes and workshops.

Unfortunately, with the worldwide growth of shibari, there has been some questionable copying or eroticizing of the cultural aesthetic of the Japanese performances and photographs — non-Japanese people wearing kimono, or rope tops only tying small Asian women as rope bottoms, for example. Instead, practice the ties, be knowledgeable about and respectful of where they come from, and make the encounter be about you and your experience.

In Japanese, "Shibari" simply means "to tie". Shibari's modern definition refers to an old Japanese aesthetic technique of rope bondage. Hojo-jutsu, a martial technique used to hold captives, is where Shibari got its start, while the local police and Samurai utilized Hojo-jutsu as a means of detention and torture in Japan between 1400 and 1700, the honor of these ancient Samurai warriors required them to treat their victims humanely. So, they used different techniques to tie their prisoners, showing the honor and status of their captured prisoner.

In the late 1800's and early 1900's a new form of erotic Hojo-justu evolved, called Kinbaku, the art of erotic bondage. In Shibari, the model is the canvas, the rope is the paint and brush, and the rigger is the rope artist.

The aesthetic arrangement of ropes and knots on the model's body in Shibari rigging emphasizes characteristics like sensuality, vulnerability, and also strength. The positioning of knots in appropriate places stimulates pressure points on the body, very similarly to acupuncture techniques and Shiatsu, a form of Japanese massage. Some believe a Shibari experience also stimulates Ki energy flow and transfer.

In addition to creating beautiful patterns, with rope, body and limb placements, Shibari rigging induces physiological conditions known as "sub space" and "top space", which are similar to the "runners high" experienced by athletes.

A Shibari experience causes a rise in endorphins and other hormones, which gives the bottom/model a trance-like sensation and the top/rigger an adrenaline rush. These effects can be seen in the model's face when a Shibari scene is done in an appropriate setting. The ecstatic state of the model following a Shibari session is sometimes fondly referred to as being "rope intoxicated."

For most practitioners of Shibari, the use of rope bondage does not include an unwilling victim like the "Damsels in Distress" images popular in Detective type magazines. Instead, there is a collaboration between the Shibari artist (the rigger/Top) and the Shibari canvas (the model/bottom) to create a combination of effects including visual beauty, power exchange, helplessness, relaxation, and sub space and top space physiological experiences.

Contemporary practitioners of Shibari enjoy creating beautiful still images, live and recorded performance art. Shibari can also be used as a component in BDSM play and an enhancement in sexual activities.

While Kinbaku-bi literally translates to "the beauty of tight binding," Kinbaku stands for "tight binding." A person is tied up using simple yet aesthetically complex patterns in the Japanese bondage technique known as kinbaku. The rope used is typically several pieces of thin rope that is between 7-8 m (23-26 ft) long, and has a diameter of around 6 mm (0.24 in) but can occasionally be as small as 4 mm (0.16 in) and is made of jute, hemp, or linen.

In Japanese this natural-fibre rope is known as asanawa. In a Western BDSM environment, stocks or manacles are used to restrain captives, and this allusion refers to the employment of hemp rope as a symbol of authority for the same purpose. [1] Sometime in the 1990s, the term "shibari" began to be often used in the West to refer to the Kinbaku bondage art. Shibari is a Japanese word that broadly means "binding" or "tying" in most contexts, but is used in BDSM to refer to this style of decorative bondage. What About The Rope?

Jute and hemp are the most popular materials used in shibari. The rope is often seven to eight meters long, four to six millimeters thick, and usually consists of three smaller strands twisted together. Natural fiber ropes have more grip, a necessary quality here — shibari doesn't use many knots, and its wrapping techniques require the rope have grip — and so are better than silk or synthetic ropes, which don't hold friction well and can also lead to faster rope burn. In my opinion, natural fiber ropes also look better and the unyielding tension feels better for the bottom.

Jute and hemp rope must be treated before use by being boiled to soften, dried under tension to keep the correct shape, singed with flame to remove the fuzzes, and oiled so it's not dry. You can buy raw rope and do this yourself, or you can buy pretreated rope. I recommend buying pretreated rope at first, but it can be fun to buy raw rope and condition it yourself in the future.

Chapter Two

Overview of Rope Types

Rope Selection & Care

Before you spend a lot of money on any type of rope, it's a good idea to explore a little and figure out the style of rope work you want to pursue and the preferences you might have. Which means, it's best to try out lots of different kinds of rope when possible ... usually by finding people who will let you check out the ropes they use?

What to buy first ...

While you're figuring out the kind of rope that's best for you to invest in, you can also buy some cheap rope just to start learning. Most hardware stores have a decent variety for not much money. Try to get something flexible and not too thick ... 4-6mm (about

1/4") and between 25 – 30 feet in length. We actually recommend cotton clothesline for your first purchase: it's cheap and easy to work with. (Note that you can often buy 50 ft. pieces that you can cut in half and get two ropes from!) You can start learning some basic knots and cuffs with that until you're ready to make the harder decisions.

Finding other rope to buy …

When you are ready to buy, "The Rope List" is a very comprehensive list of vendors that is updated regularly.

A Guide to Selection

Just because everyone at your local rope group is using "rope type x" doesn't mean you need to use it. Consider the advantages and disadvantages of each option carefully, practice handling and tying with some examples, speak with your tying partners, and then make an informed choice. Some specific things to consider:

Strength – Does the strength of the rope matter to you? If you don't plan on doing suspension work, it may not be a factor. [Note: thicker rope is stronger rope.]

Grip – How do you feel about the grip and knotting characteristics? Rope that grips on itself really well is great for holding frictions, but that sometimes means it's also difficult to untie. If a knot gets stuck, how calmly are you able to deal with that? Do you mind cutting your rope? (Hint: you shouldn't where safety is involved!) [Note: thicker rope can sometimes reduce grip in practical terms.]

Handling – Do you like how it handles and feels in your hands? For tops, this will be important, but can be a very subjective characteristic. Think of terms like: heavy / light, springy / floppy, supple / stiff, etc.

[Note: thicker rope can be less pliant and more difficult to handle.]

Feel – Do you like how it feels on your skin and around your body? For tops, this will mainly affect wear-and-tear on your hands. For bottoms, this will likely be important everywhere ... and probably matters more! Some bottoms prefer rope that feels soft and comfortable, some enjoy the bite of harder, scratchier rope. Some can't stand the "industrial" feel of MFP, some break out in hives from jute. Speaking of ...

Allergies – Are you or your partners allergic to it? This is important to know before you have someone wrapped up in the stuff! People with grass allergies probably won't want to tie with jute or hemp, for example.

Aesthetics – Do you like how it looks? While this may seem trivial, this can actually matter a lot to some tops and bottoms, particularly if they practice decorative bondage or enjoy taking photographs of their rope work.

Materials

In the bondage world, rope falls into two main categories: synthetic or natural fiber. The types of rope you'll likely see most often are hemp and jute (natural fiber) or nylon (synthetic), though there's a wide range of others.

Natural-Fiber Rope

Natural-fiber rope in general tends to be weaker and less durable than synthetic rope, but usually offers better grip, easier handling, and less chance for rope burn. In addition, natural-fiber tends to have a lot of variation in its construction, so its strength and durability can vary widely depending on the source and manufacturer. If you advance beyond Rope 101 and eventually decide you want to practice suspension, you will need to carefully weigh the pros and cons of using natural-fiber rope for that purpose given its weaker nature.

Hemp (medium strength – 400-500*): soft, knots easily, easier to care for than jute, slightly stronger than jute

Linen (medium strength, similar to hemp): softer than hemp, knots fairly easily, machine-washable

Jute (weak – 200-300*): springier and lighter than hemp and linen, knots well, unties well, difficult to care for (though many use it for suspension, many others argue against this due to its weakness and the inherent variability depending on construction)

Cotton (weak to medium strength, but varies by make): soft, knots easily, but is difficult to untie; not recommended for suspension due to its knotting (and stretch for some makes, though this can vary widely); cheaper cotton is very weak

Bamboo/Rayon and Silk (medium strength, similar to hemp): typically the softest of the ropes (so, good for bedroom bondage), knots easily, but the stretch makes it unsuitable for suspension; also expensive

Sisal, Manila (weak, similar to jute): rough and scratchy, good for sadistic play, but not for loading at bondage diameters

Coconut (weakest): rough and scratchy, good for sadistic play, but easily breakable and not suited for other purposes

* All ratings are approximate, given in pounds of force at 6mm. Natural fiber ropes are typically not rated for load/breaking strength, so use at your own risk. Carefully inspect and test natural-fiber ropes and use only with informed consent of all parties.

Synthetic Rope

Synthetic rope's biggest advantage is its strength and durability. Synthetic rope also tends to be easier to clean and care for. However, it also tends to be more difficult to work with because it doesn't usually hold frictions as well, can be slippery or stiff, and more easily causes rope burn.

Nylon (very strong – 1200-1500*): soft, little grip, stretchy, can be dyed, machine-washable [note: because of how slippery nylon can be, we typically don't recommend this for beginners]

MFP/Polypropylene (strong – 1100-1300*): can be stiffer than nylon, less stretch, little grip, floats in water, can't be dyed at home, UV resistant, machine-washable

Polyester (strong, similar to MFP): stiffer, less grip, less stretch, machine-washable

Synthetic "Natural Fiber" [typically sold as Hempex or POSH] (moderately strong – 750-1100*): looks like natural fiber, stiffer, lighter, better grip than other synthetics, machine washable

* All ratings are approximate, given in pounds of force at 6mm.

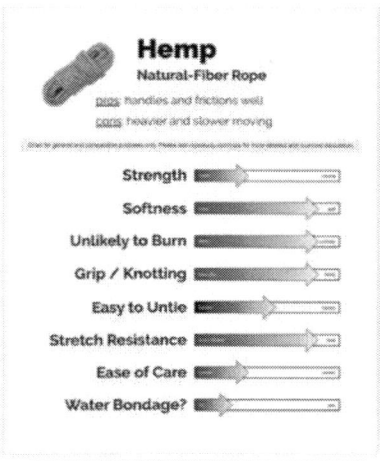 

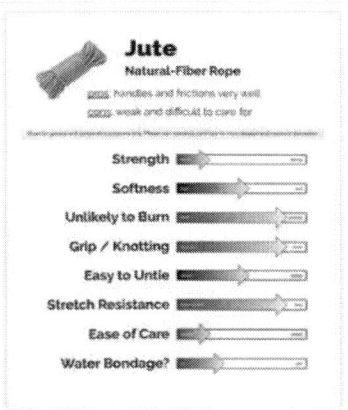 

HEMP

Hemp – Is one of the most commonly used types of rope in modern shibari. Some of the great things about hemp are it's rough texture enables you to create knots that are tightened by friction. In other words, the rope will not slide as easily and your knots will hold better.

Its lack of elasticity which means that the rope will not be deformed under tension and the tightness of your knots can be controlled with your hands.

The rope width can be really thin which is great for aesthetically pleasing knots. I highly recommend it if you are doing performances or photoshoots.

If you buy hemp by the bulk it will come untreated and will be very rough, I recommend buying rope that is already treated and ready for rope bondage. There are plenty of shops online where you can buy it.

Cotton

- It is also rather usual to see cotton. One important aspect of cotton is its low cost. The cost of a comprehensive rope bondage kit can be very high.

- It is more comfortable to wear because it is softer than hemp.

- Because it takes a lot of speed or pressure to create rope burn, it is excellent for novices.

- When washed, it gets even softer.

- You can color it as you like because it is really simple to dye.

- It is quite easy to dye, so you can give it any color you want. Additionally, it is quite lightweight, making it easy to transport a lot of rope.

- On the negative side, unlike hemp, it is elastic and extends when put under tension. Due to this, it is challenging to manage how tightly the knots are tied and to untie them. Make sure you have your shears handy because it can get a bit frustrating.

- Cotton rope can feel abrasive when dry because cotton does not absorb lubricating oil.

Where Do You Buy Rope?

[Esinem Rope](#) (This is my favorite place to buy rope and the only place which carries linen hemp, which I love.)

[Jade Rope](#)

[Twisted Monk](#)

[Erin Houdini](#)

[Kankinawa.com](#)

[My Nawashi (Etsy)](#)

Construction

As with everything else in this section, we have to speak in generalities, particularly when it comes to natural fiber rope, because there can be so much variation depending on the manufacturer.

In general, you'll find two types of rope: twisted or braided. Natural fiber bondage rope is typically twisted while synthetic may be twisted or braided.

Twisted rope is usually made of three strands, and each strand is created by spinning together the yarns of the fiber making the rope. Single-ply rope is created by using single yarns, twisted together, to form each strand. Double-ply rope is created by first twisting together two single yarns and then twisting those "doubled-yarns" together to form the strands.

Single-ply rope tends to be more flexible and easier to work with and tends to make more compact frictions, but it's more susceptible to wear. Double-ply rope is a little stiffer and bulkier, but also a little more durable.

Braided rope not specifically made for bondage tends to have a solid core of some type (either the same or different fiber). This core adds bulk and makes the rope less pliable. Many people remove this core before using the rope for bondage, which makes the rope easier to work with but can also weaken the rope to varying amounts.

Rope Ends

Rope ends can be finished with a number of different knots or other options, including:

- Knotted: the easiest and most common in natural fiber rope; often preferred because it makes joining ropes easier; common finishing knots include overhand, flat overhand, wall knot, Mathew Walker knot, and thistle knot.

- Whipped: twine is used to secure the end; makes it easier to pull rope through, but more difficult to join; often used for specialty rope, like thin detail rope for hair, etc.

- Taped: similar to whipped, but using tape to secure the ends; more often used on synthetic rope than natural fiber

- Fused: synthetic rope ends can be melted and fused together; similar advantages and disadvantages to whip ends; sometimes combined with taped ends.

Size

Diameter

Typical bondage rope is between 5mm and 8mm in diameter, with 6mm being the most common. However, it's worth noting that the diameter of natural fiber rope is usually more of an approximation.

Although thinner ropes are more flexible, allow for tighter knots to be tied, and retain knots better, they are also weaker and require more effort to untie. In addition, tighter knots cause the rope to bite into the flesh more uncomfortably. The knots that thicker ropes form are bulkier and may be simpler to untie, but they are stronger and sometimes more pleasant.

Length

Most rope made for bondage is sold in 7 or 8 meter lengths (23 to 26 feet). However, you can also order or make custom-length rope depending on your needs. One typical recommendation for rope length is "four arm-pulls" ... in other words, if you measure your arm from armpit to fingertip, and then multiply that distance by 4, that's a good "ideal" rope length for the rope top. Another way to find an ideal length is to consider the size of the person or people being tied and the amount of rope required for the types of ties they're used to. However, this isn't always practical if you're not making or cutting your own rope, as it often requires special orders (which can cost more).

Many rope tops prefer using ropes of the same length and simply joining additional ropes as needed. Shorter ropes mean joining more frequently, and longer ropes mean more rope to pull through for every move. However, shorter ropes can be handy for finishing a tie that only needs a little more rope to complete, and longer ropes can be useful for specific purposes or larger bodies.

Common Lengths

For the "main" ropes: 7-8 meters / 25 to 30 feet (these aren't strictly equivalent measurements, but are typical lengths)

For smaller ropes (for finishing, extending, etc.): 3-4 meters / 10 to 15 feet or shorter

Typical Number of Ropes:

For beginners: 3 main ropes to start with are usually enough

For intermediate: 6 main ropes and at least 1 smaller rope

For advanced: 8+ main ropes and 2-5 smaller ropes

Rope & Style

One other thing to consider before paying much for rope is the style of rope you want to pursue. We considered these styles in an earlier lesson, but below are some quick notes on how three of these styles relate to rope selection. However, please note that there are no "rules" for which ropes "must" be used with any particular style ... just common uses and preferences.

Western – This type of rope work lends itself well to nylon, cotton, hemp, and other thicker, softer types of rope.

Common Material: nylon, cotton, or hemp

Common Size: 30+ feet (usually folded in half for use), 6-8+mm in diameter

Japanese – This type of rope work lends itself well to jute and hemp (mainly because of the friction and grip of natural fiber rope), and typically avoids synthetic rope altogether.

Common Material: jute or hemp

Common Size: 20-30 feet (typically folded in half for use), 4-6mm in diameter (4mm usually referred to as "hojo" rope for specialized tying)

Decorative – A wide range of different rope types might be used for this approach, though colored rope and rope of different sizes that allows for more detailed, intricate knots and patterns are typically preferred.

Common Material: MFP, nylon, cotton

Common Size: varies widely depending on the design of the decorative tie

When you must have gotten the above criteria correct, one can look at trying the basics as stated below, pay attention to the pictures and try and make them yourself. You are finally ready to begin tying!

Chapter Three

Basic Knots

First things first. In these lessons we will go over the basic knots that you will use in most of your ties. This is a great way for you to familiarize yourself with your ropes. These will be your tools and will allow you to be creative and perform your own ties in the future.

You will learn the following knots:

- Overhand
- Overhand on a Bite
- Square
- Lark's head
- Two half hitches
- Crossing hitch
- Double coin

- Inline double coin

- Fisherman's knot

- Prusik head

- Inline prusik head

- Have fun tying!

In knot tying, a bight is the bent or slack portion of a rope, thread, or yarn between the two ends. A knot is referred regarded as being in the bight if it can only be tied using the rope's bight and cannot access the ends. The term "bight" is also used in a more specific way when describing turk's head knot, indicating how many repetitions of braiding are made in the circuit of a given knot.

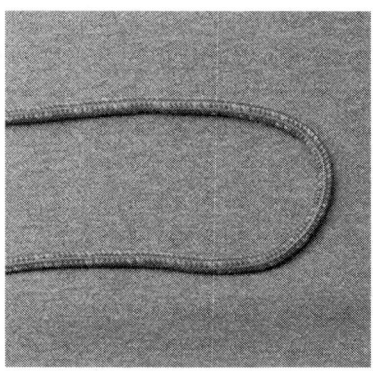

Bight Vs. Open Loop

Sources differ on whether an open loop or U-shaped curve in a rope qualifies as a bight. Jennifer treats bights and loops as distinct, stating that a curve "no narrower than a semicircle" is a bright, while an open loop is a curve "narrower than a bight but with separated ends". However, The Illustrated Encyclopedia of Knots (2002) states: "Any section of line that is bent into a U-shape is a bight."

Slipped knot

In order to make a slipped knot (also slipped loop and quick release knot), a bight must be passed, rather than the end. This slipped form of the knot is more easily untied. A reef knot is all that is required to tie the classic bow knot for tying shoelaces, with the final overhand knot being done with two bights rather than the ends. Similar to how a slipped clove hitch is a slippery hitch.

In the bight

In the bight (or on a bight) refers to the act of tying a knot within a bight of line. This specifically indicates that the knot can be made without having access to the rope's ends. This might be a crucial characteristic for knots to have when the rope's ends are out of reach, such as when creating a fixed loop in the center of a lengthy climbing rope.

Numerous knots that are typically tied with an end also come in forms that are tied in the bight (for example, the bowline and the bowline on a bight). In other instances, a knot being tied in the bight is a matter of technique rather than a distinction in the knot's finished form. When the clove hitch is being cast onto a closed ring, which requires access to a rope end, it cannot be produced "in the bight" but can only be done when it is being slipped over the end of a post. It is impossible to tie some knots, like the overhand knot, in the bight without altering their final shape.

Examples are as follows;

The blue rope (right) is half-hitched through and around a bight of the red rope (left) in this sheet bend.

The final tuck of this slipped buntline hitch is made with a bight rather than the end, making it easier to release after tightening.

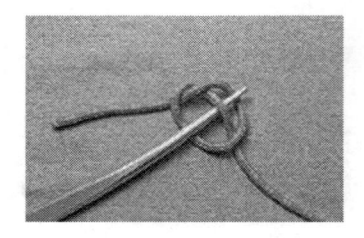

In the tying of a marlinespike hitch, a bight of the standing part is snagged through the loop.

The bights, in the case of this 3-lead 10-bight Turk's head knot, are the scallops along the perimeter of the knot.

An overhand knot tied in the bight results in an overhand loop.

Overhand on a Bight

Overhand knot

Bight goes over tail on bight side of wrap

Standing end runs perpendicular to wraps

Bight and standing end keep direction but lend themselves to a 90 rotation

Requires another knot to secure

Lark's Head

This knot is the building block for most ties ranging from the easiest to the most complex

Square Knot

Pay attention when tying this knot. It looks simple, but it's easy to end up with a grandma's knot if tied incorrectly.

Prusik Head Knot

This knot will tighten under tension and remain loose when not

One-handed Slip Knot

Impress your friends by tying a one-handed slip-knot in less than 5 seconds!

Prusik Head Inline Knot

Attach two ropes with ease

Cross Hitch Friction

Keep the ropes in place using friction

Double Coin Knot

Join two ropes in an elegant way

Inline Double Coin Knot

A beautiful knot. Great for decorative ties

A single-column tie is probably the most common shibari tie. A column is a thing you're tying: a leg, a waist, a chair rung, a bed post. Below, I'll demonstrate on an arm. Make sure your bottom takes off any wrist jewelry/watches first.

First, find the bight (center) of your rope. Wrap it around the wrist (above the joint) twice, leaving room for a couple fingers to slip between the rope and the wrist. Cross the bight over the working ends (the two ends of rope opposite the bight).

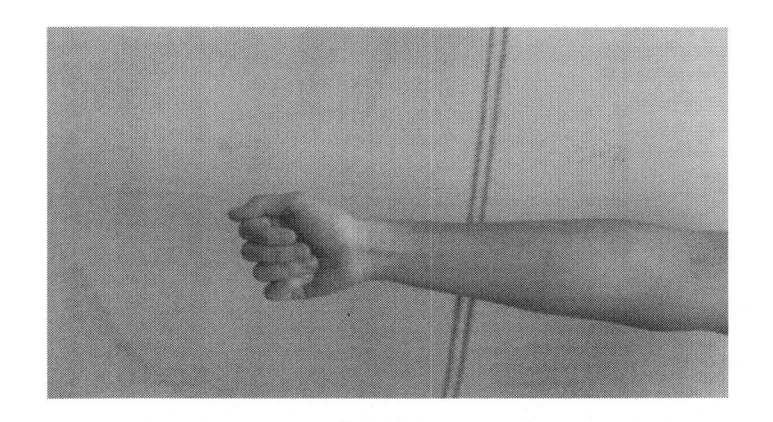

Tuck the bight underneath all the ropes. It's better to always reach under and pull rope instead of pushing it through because it'll retain its lay (twist pattern) better and not get out of shape.

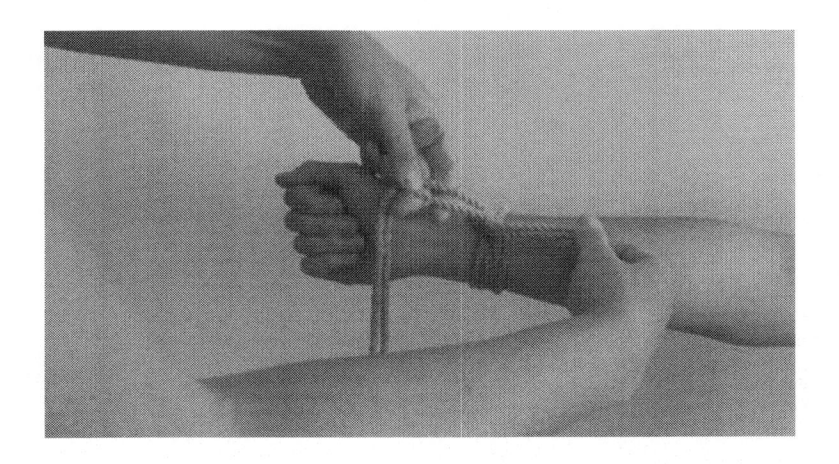

Make a loop with the working end and pull the bight through. If the result does not create a knot and just falls apart, try bringing the bight through the other side.

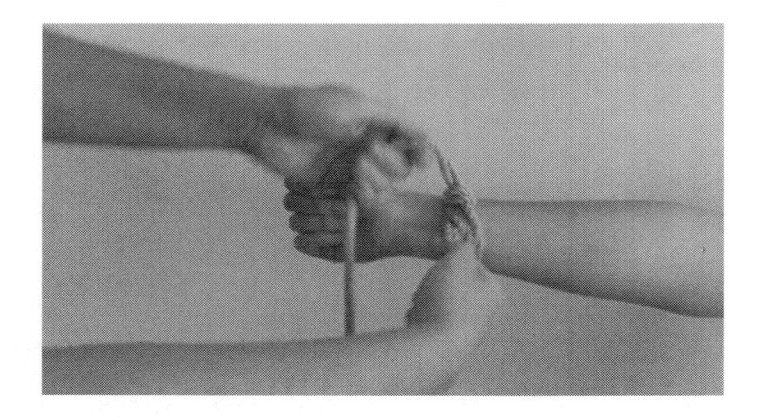

Create yet another loop and bring the bight through again. Pull tight on the knot — it shouldn't tighten on the wrist at all, and you should still be able to slip a couple of fingers between the ropes and the wrist. That's it!

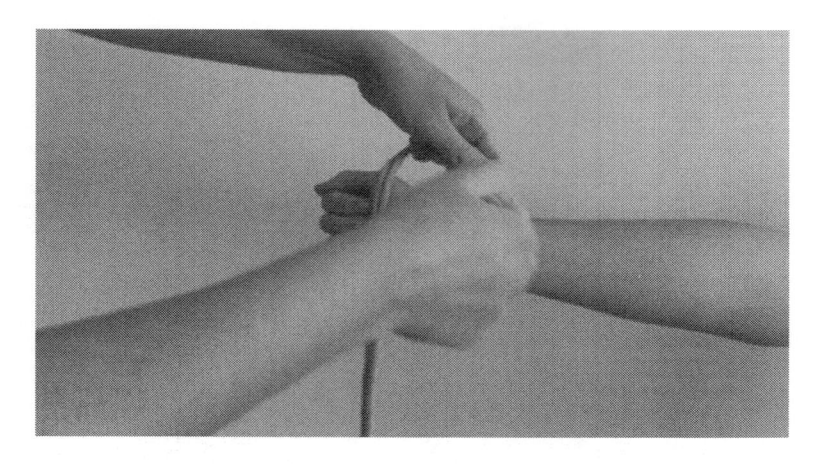

Remember:

There should be room to move the wrist within the shibari tie, but not enough to slip the hand out of the tie. You should be able to slide a couple fingers underneath the ropes.

There should still be some length of bight left, to keep the knot from coming undone. It's better to have a bit too long of a leftover bight loop as a beginner — you can work up to having it look trim and perfect after you master the tie.

The four ropes along the wrist should not twist or overlap each other, as this would create too much pressure in one spot.

The tie isn't at the very end of the wrist but instead is a couple inches up from the hand and the knot is on the outside of the wrist, not on the sensitive inner wrist, to reduce chances of nerve damage.

Using The Bight As A Pulley

In order to safely attach your bottom to something else without putting undue strain on the ropes around your wrist, the knot, or the wrist itself, you can also use the bight as a pulley system. If you do tie overhead, make sure your bottom supports their weight and doesn't hang from their wrists, since this could seriously harm their nerves. This is not a healthy manner to hold weight.

To utilize the bight as a pulley, thread the rope through it after wrapping the ends of the rope around a hardpoint (usually a hook or loop in the ceiling you can tie to), a bed post, or anything else comes to mind.

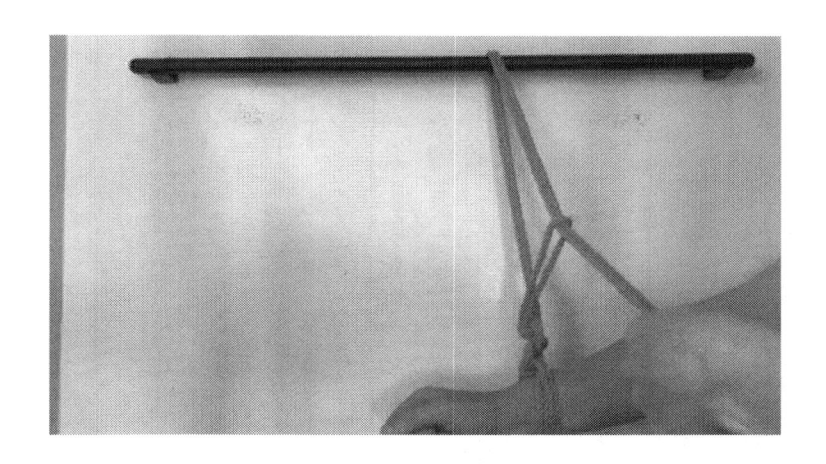

Double-Column Shibari Tie

A double column ties two columns together. I'll demonstrate here on two wrists, but you can tie a wrist to an ankle, an ankle to a chair leg, a wrist to a thigh, and a wrist to an upper arm with the arm folded, rendering the arm unable to be used, or an ankle to an upper thigh with the knee bent.

Start by finding the bight or center of your rope. Wrap it around both wrists twice. Make sure to leave a lot more slack on your bight than you did for the single column tie.

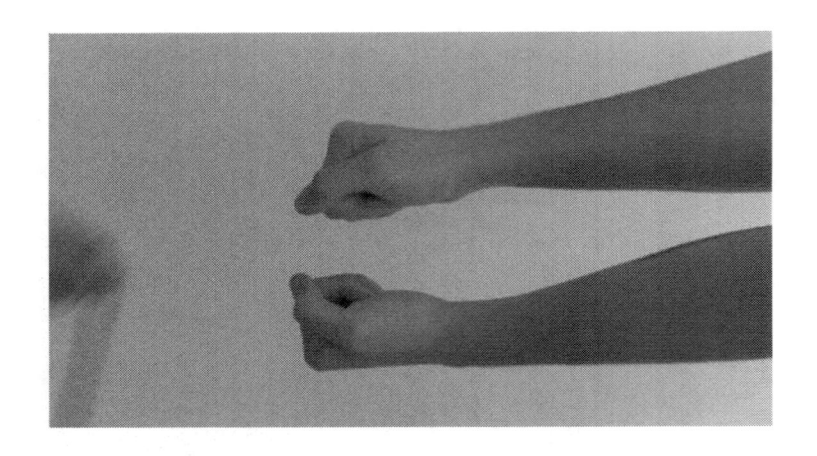

Cross the bight over the working ends at the top and center of the wrists. Pass the rope through the wrists and behind both sets of the ropes and then back to the front. Unlike the single-column tie, which just wraps the bight under the top set of ropes, the double-column tie wraps the bight over both the top and bottom sets of ropes. The rope goes between the two columns, over both sets of ropes, and back up again.

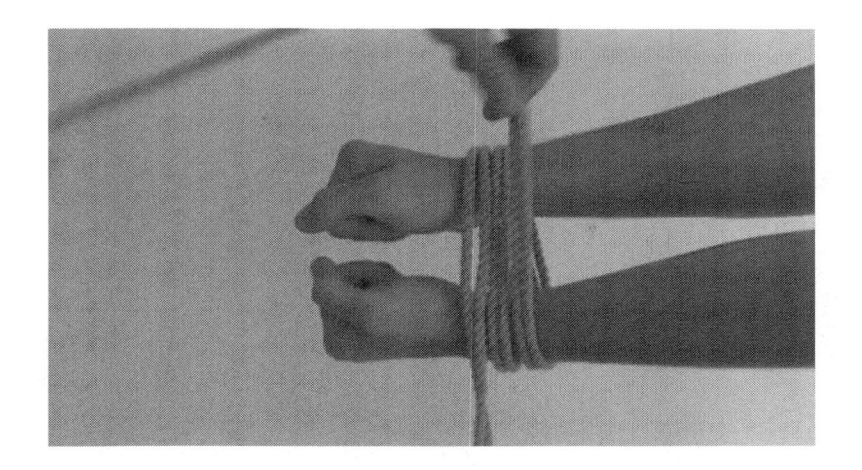

Make a loop with the working end and bring the bight through. If it does not create a knot and just falls apart, try bringing the bight through the other side.

Create yet another loop and bring the bight through again. Pull tight to lock the knots. The knot should not tighten on the wrists at all, and you should still be able to slip a couple fingers between the ropes and the wrists, but not so loose that the hands can slip through.

Chapter Four

Chest Harness

In shibari, a chest harness can stand alone or act as a base to secure other ties. This version is simple, but you can get more complicated and decorative with it once you learn it.

First, positions the bight at the center of your bottom's back, and wraps the rope once around your bottom below the chest and draw the working ends through the bight. Make sure the part that crosses over is in the middle of the back on their spine. The ropes should be snug, but not so snug your bottom can't breathe.

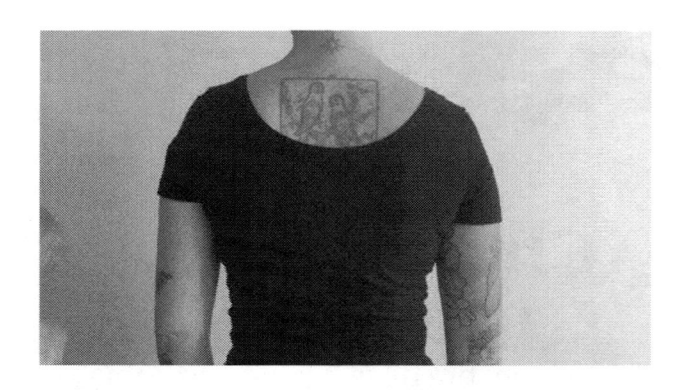

Bring the working ends back around the front of their body again, going in the opposite direction. If you don't switch directions the rope won't stay tight and will fall off the body. When you get back to the center of the back again, pull the working ends up through the loop you just created on the opposite side of where you pulled the rope from — the side with the doubled-over rope. Make sure the ropes are not crossed and line up neatly.

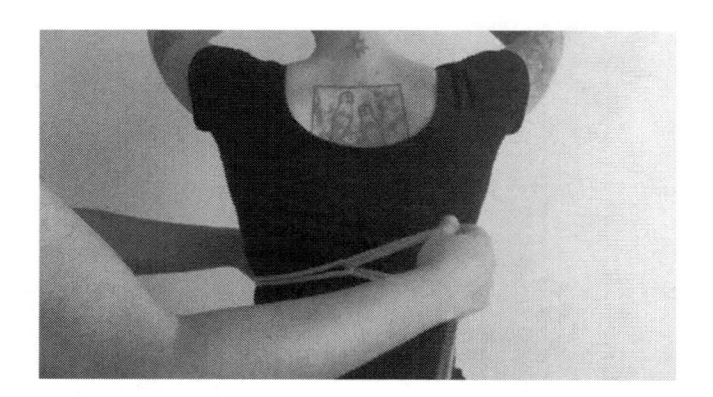

Reverse direction again and bring the working ends around the body one more time, this time above the chest. Wrap the working ends underneath the rope stem (in this case, the section of rope that goes vertical along the spine).

Reverse direction around the body one last time, making sure your ropes are above the previous wrap of ropes and lay flat and neat. Bring the working ends through the loop created by reversing direction — the side with the doubled-over rope.

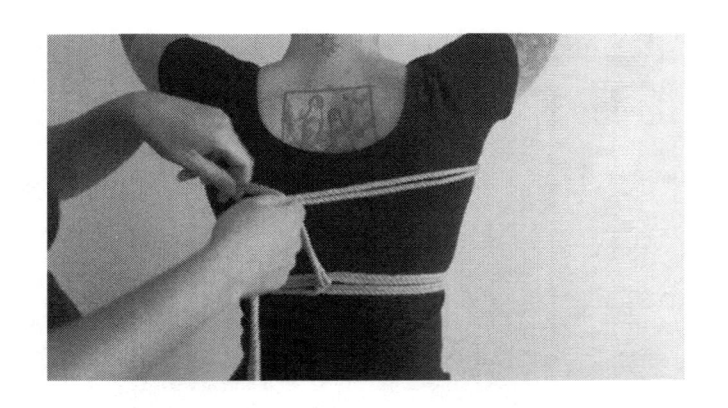

Take the working ends and bring them over the shoulder to the front of your bottom, and bring them over the top ropes in front then under the bottom ropes. Pinch the bottom ropes together so they don't lose their shape while you reverse direction with the working ends. Bring them back up and under the second top ropes. You'll probably need to extend the rope at some point here (see the bottom of the page.) Make sure the knot is in a comfortable place for the bottom. You can move the knot a bit down the first rope if not.

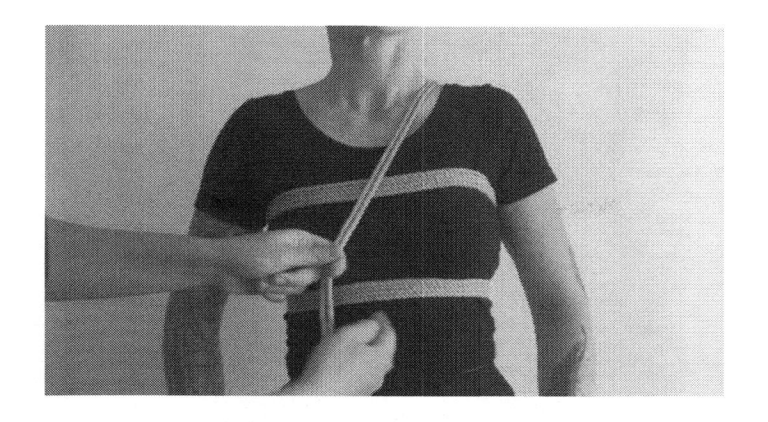

Bring the working ends over the other shoulder and around to the back of your bottom. Pass them over the top right ropes, and up diagonally between the top left ropes and the left shoulder rope, as shown.

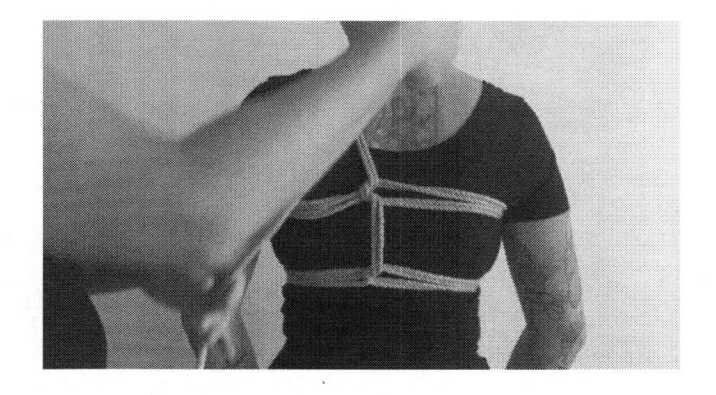

Bring the working ends over both shoulder ropes, and under the right top ropes.

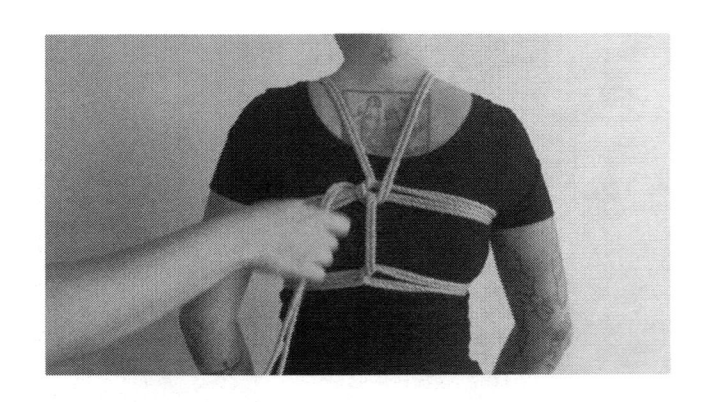

Make a half hitch on the stem. A half hitch is made by making a loop in the working ends, bringing the ropes over the stem, behind the stem, and back through the loop. Pull to tighten. You can wrap your excess rope around the stem, and/or weave it up the shoulder ropes in a figure-eight weave, or leave the rope length to tie to an additional arm or leg tie, or tie it to a hard point (not for suspension) Start a leg tie, which will immobilize one leg, by tying a single column tie on the ankle. It looks cleaner if you start the single column tie by spiraling the bight down the ankle, instead of up, so the working ends are on top. Once you've tied the single column, push the bottom's shin to bring the ankle as close to the lower thigh as you can. (Note that, because it leaves most of your body and your arms free, this is a really fun tie to practice on yourself.) The muscles of the leg will relax as the bottom sits in this tie, and often the ropes will get slackly and loose if you do not do this step.

Next, spiral the working ends up the leg, making sure the first wrap is low on the thigh. Depending on the size of your bottom's leg you can do anywhere between two to four wraps here (you can also extend rope and do as many as you want!). You can try with three as shown, and if you find you have run out of rope before the tie is done, back up and try with two, etc., or if you have too much left over rope, back up and try with four.

Pass the final rope of your spiral over itself on the inside of the knee. Bring your finger through the triangle you just created, and grab the rope and pull underneath. Use your other hand to pinch where the ropes cross so they don't slide. Take the working ends and bring them over the top rope, and then under the left rope.

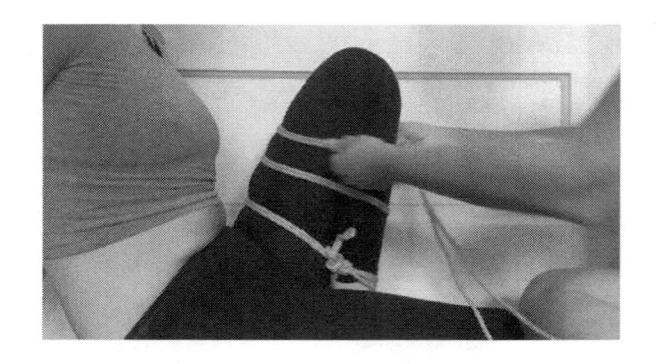

Repeat this knot on each rope working down the spiral, including the bottom rope. Pass the working ends through the leg and around to the other side.

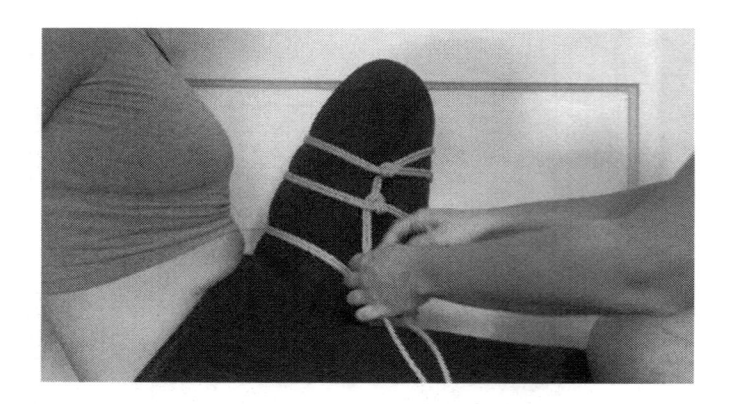

On the outside of the leg now, pull the working ends to cinch tight. You're going to repeat this knot again on the outside of the leg, but this time backwards, as your working ends are now running up the leg instead of down. Bring the working ends up over the bottom rope, back down on the right, then over the bottom rope, and back up under the left.

Repeat this step on each rope of the spiral until you get to the top.

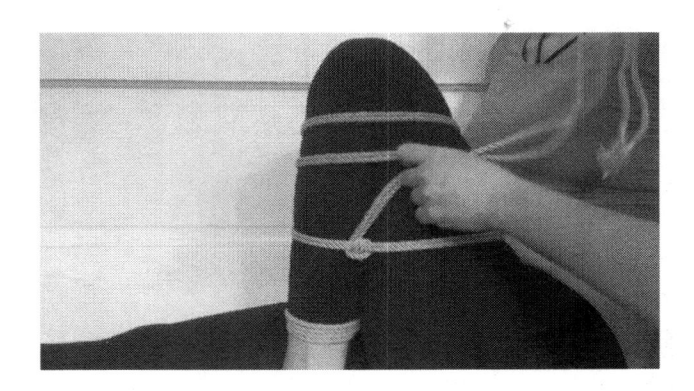

On the top rope's knot, finish it off by bringing the working ends through the loop, so they reverse direction and go back down the leg again.

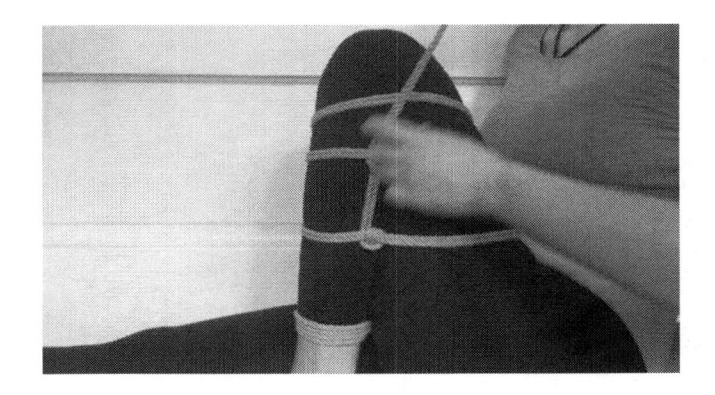

If you have leftover rope, you can twist it around the stem. Tie it off with a hitch and tuck the ropes around the stem or between the legs.

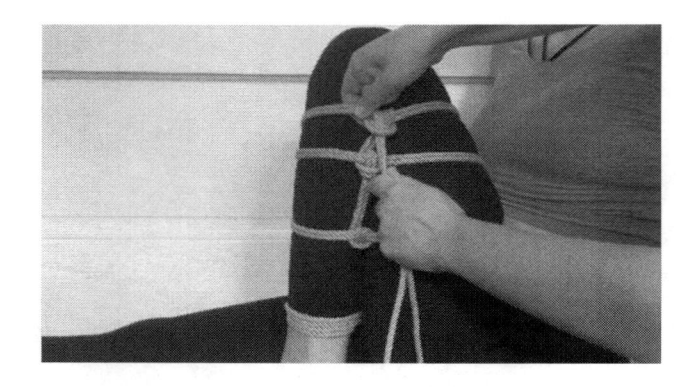

You will be faced with a situation where you will need to extend the rope for the desired bond, below is an illustration on how to go about it

Extending Rope

You'll need to extend rope when you run out. This is one of several ways to do this.

With your second rope, make a loop with your hand by putting your hand inside the bight, grasping the ropes, and pulling the bight over your hand. You'll have a loop, which is called a lark's head knot.

Put the first rope's ends into the lark's head and tighten. If your ropes have knots at the end, you can bring the lark's head knot down to the knots and stop here. If you have whipped ends, or you feel like it, continue to the next step.

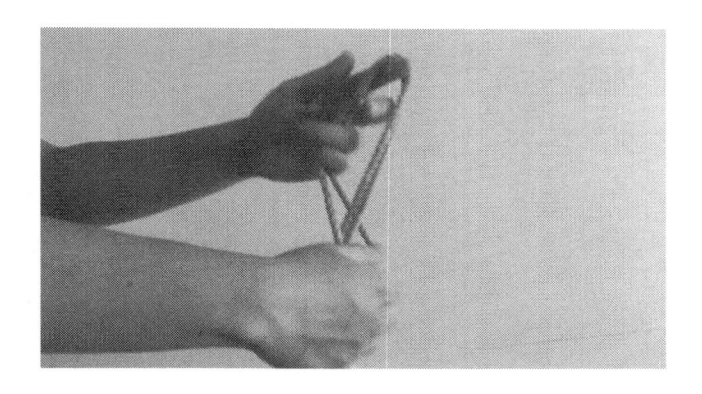

Make sure the lark's head is not at the very end of your first rope, and there's about 5"/12cm of ends left. Bring both sides of the first rope together and roll the knot up.

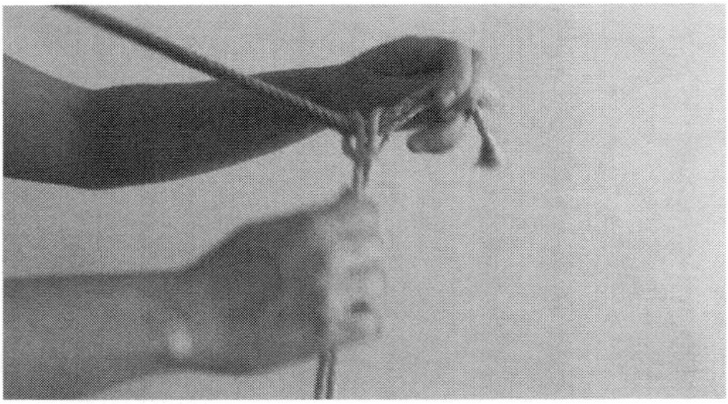

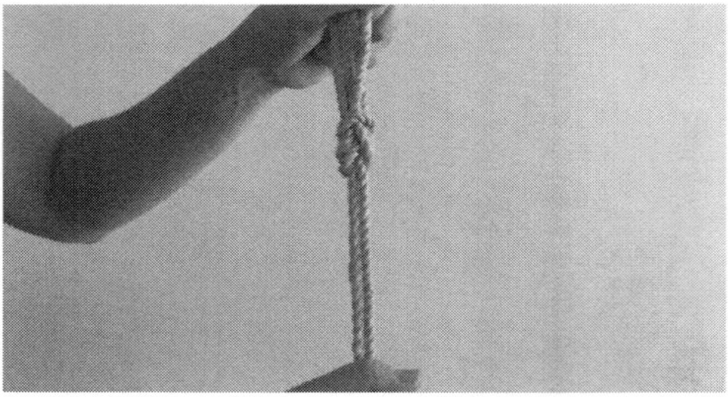

Chapter Five

How To Tie Rope Armbinder

This one is about how to tie an armbinder, using the classic "arms behindthe back" version. There are a few different uses for this tie.

My Favorite Way Of Tying Wrists

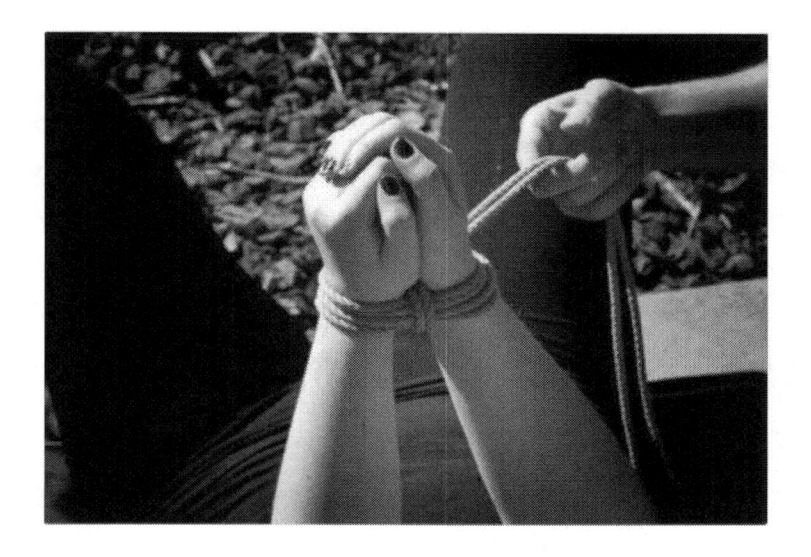

There's tying wrists, and then there's tying wrists in such a way that it's prettier, more inescapable, and pretty much guaranteed not to tighten down on your partner.

All of which I'm a fan of.

Now I'm going to share my favorite way of doing that.Often, when people tie wrists, they leave the knot on top of the wrists.

This isn't generally a problem; because you're tying a nice, obedient person who's looking forward to all the good times. Other times, you're tying someone who's going to be pesky and try to escape, for whatever reason.

And that's when having a knot on top becomes a problem; because that means that the person tied up can easily reach the knot with their teeth, and proceed to wreak havoc on it.

The fact that the knot is on top of the wrists also means that it just doesn't look as clean and tidy as it could; while looks aren't that important during play, it's still nice to have good looking ties on other occasions, like when you're leading someone around at a party, doing ceremonial or aesthetic rope bondage, whatever.

So it's good to have another way of doing things.

Here's the recipe:

Step One: The Position

grasp your rope bottom firmly by the wrists, bring their hands together in front of their chest, and using their joined wrists as a handle, push them firmly down onto their back, so that they're now lying down. This presents the bottom of their wrists to your convenience, and also has the added advantage of giving the scene a very assertive, directive flavor right from the beginning.

(Pro-Tip: Telling the person you're tying to put their elbows together will make your life easier; this means you're tying a column, as opposed to a triangle. Learning this saved me a lot of hassle.)

Step Two: The Tie

Begin wrapping the rope forward over their wrists. I like to wrap moving up the forearms, away from the wrists.

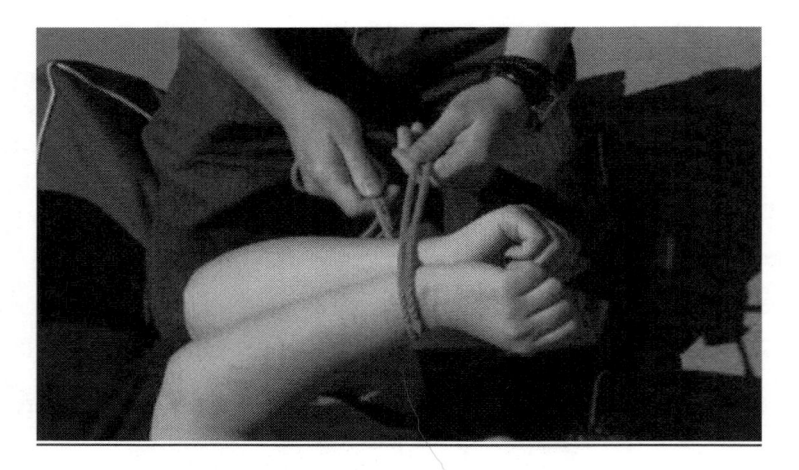

Make sure you get at least two lengths of doubled rope over their wrists.

Once you've done that, bring both ends of rope upward. And now cross them over.

Pro-Tip the second: if you don't have enough room to wiggle the bight between her wrists (or under the bands, later on) they're too close together. Give yourself a little slack and tell the person you're tying to separate their wrists a little more. It helps a LOT.

Note: the bight (middle of the rope) is to the right in this picture

The bight goes underneath ALL of the wraps. That's the top set, and the bottom set on the other side of the wrists.

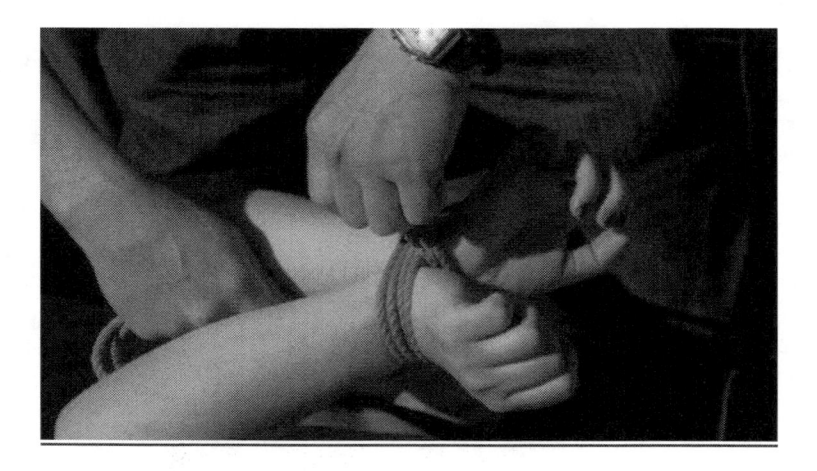

While the other hand forms a loop by making a simple twist.

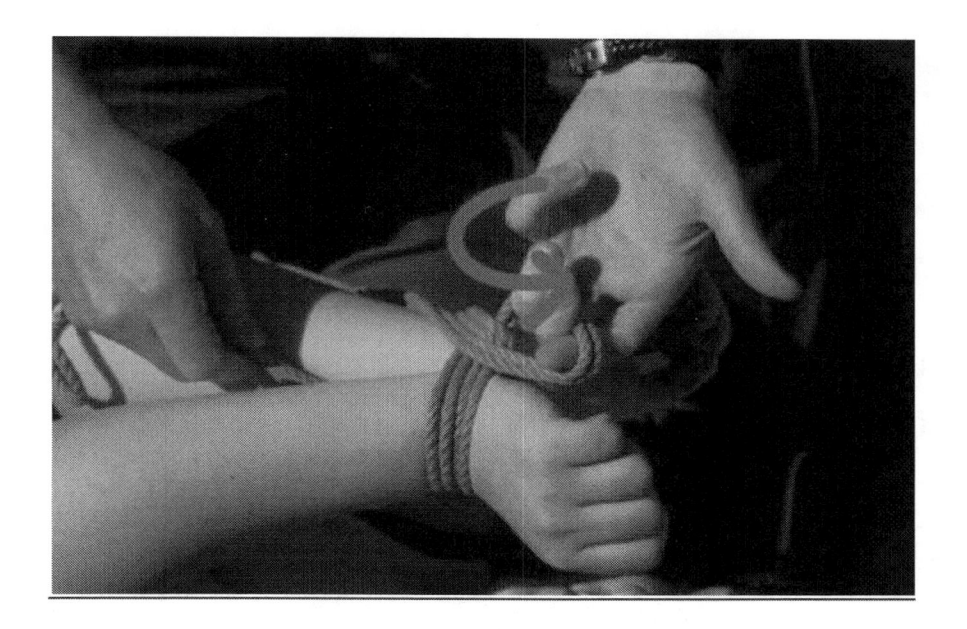

Make sure the trailing end of rope stays roughly where it is in this picture, to the inside of the loop

The bight, marked with arrows in this picture, then goes through the loop I made in the previous picture, and then under just the TOP set of wraps, on this side of the wrist.

It helps to pull the bight under, as opposed to pushing; I generally stick a finger under the wraps and hook the bight through like a crochet hook. Much smoother and more efficient action.

Now put the bight through the loop again, for the last time (it's now gone through the loop twice).

And tighten down. This is mostly accomplished by pulling the trailing end at the top of the photo, which tightens down the knot and holds it closed.

Ta da! A clean, flat, compact knot, which I have never seen collapse, and which won't tighten down on your partners wrists after it's finished. It's a variant of a bowline, closely related to the Summerville Bowline, Strugglers Knot, and Burlington Bowline. All of which are built on the same principles. All the tightening goes to just that top band of rope, so it's not pinching both bottom and top bands of rope together too much and the wrists aren't being badly compressed.

I've been told by someone I tie a lot that this is actually quite comfortable, too; more so than double overhand or "twisty knots" which are sometimes used for the same purpose.

And the final result looks so damn pretty. All clean and smooth and nice looking. Mom, that there's a a good looking set of bound wrists. She rather likes the way it looks, too.

How to create hogtie;

we're going to take two ties we've learned before and combine them into a hogtie. A hogtie places your bottom on the floor, face down, in either a chest harness (which we learned already) or a box tie which includes the wrists. Then, the ankles are secured to the chest ties and pulled in tightly. This tie is safer than tying the ankles to the wrists in a more Western-style hogtie as the weight of the legs is distributed across the chest instead of putting pressure on the sensitive wrists. You can either do a simple double-column tie on the ankles, or get more decorative with tying both legs into the leg tie we learned earlier.

Start by tying a chest harness on your bottom. Be sure when you extend rope for this tie that you don't have any knots right in the sternum or areas on the chest that might hurt once your bottom lies chest-down. Lay your bottom down on their belly. If you'd like to incorporate their arms, both use a new rope or the ends of the leftover rope from the chest harness and tie a single column tie around the wrists. Make sure the inside of their wrists are touching to keep the sensitive inner wrists protected. Then, tie a double column tie on their ankles.

Next, take the ends of the ankle ropes and pass them through the center column (spine) of the chest harness. Go over and do not include the ropes used to tie the wrists (if tied), so that pressure isn't being applied to the wrist tie.

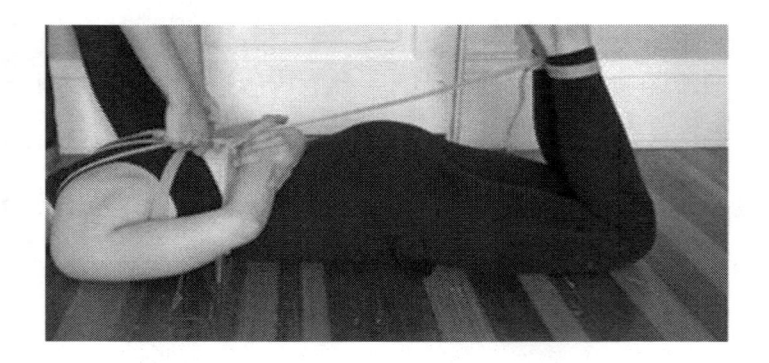

Then go back and loop the rope through the bight at the ankle, and around back through the center column/spine again.

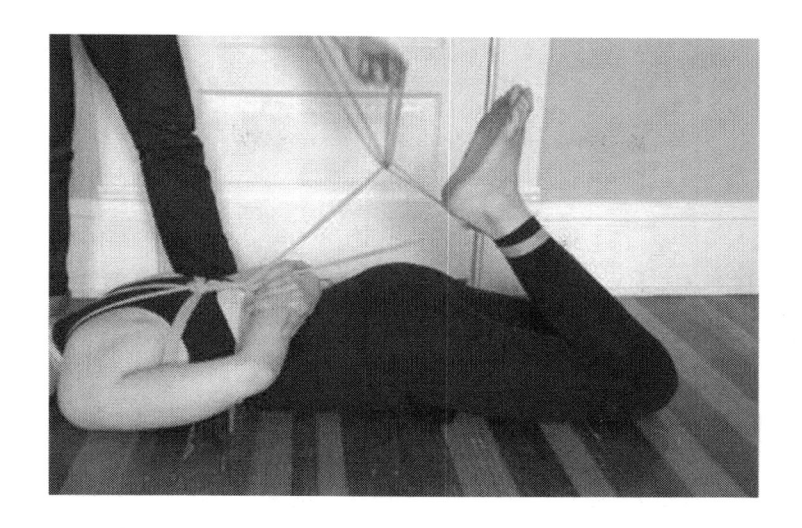

Tighten the tie until snug, but don't make sure your bottom isn't overextended and super uncomfortable. Tie off with a half hitch.

And secure with another half hitch.

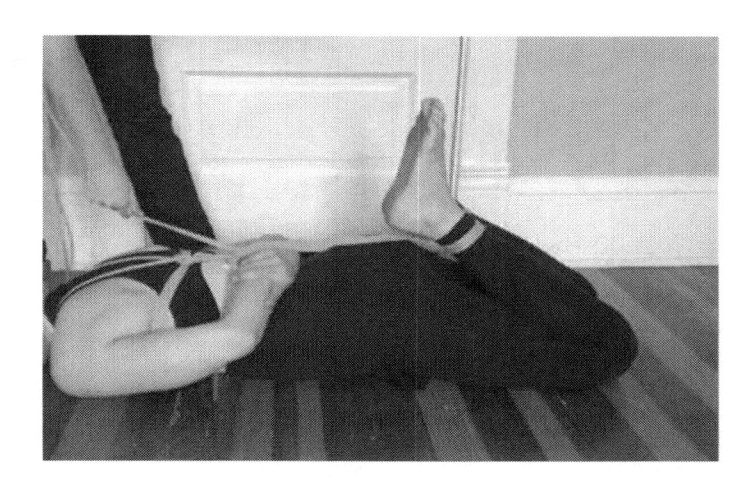

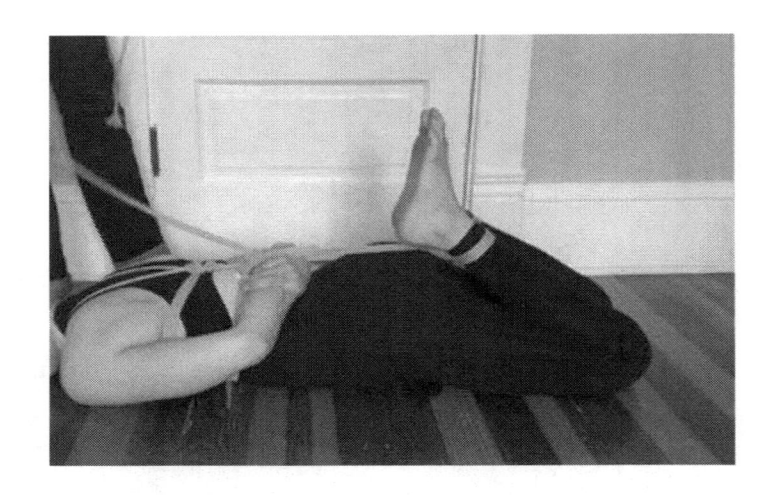

If you find the rope places too much pressure on the wrists, you can try tying it around the top of the chest harness instead. Pass the ropes behind both shoulder ropes, right above the top knot, and tie off the same way.

You'll need a new rope to knot a single column tie around both ankle ropes to the chest harness if you want to be more aesthetically pleasing and use leg ties rather than the double column tie. Using the same pulley technique as the tie above, attach that new rope to the chest harness. To avoid tying the legs together, you can even use two different ropes to bind the ankles apart.

How To Create The Armbinder:

Start with a double column tie around the wrists.

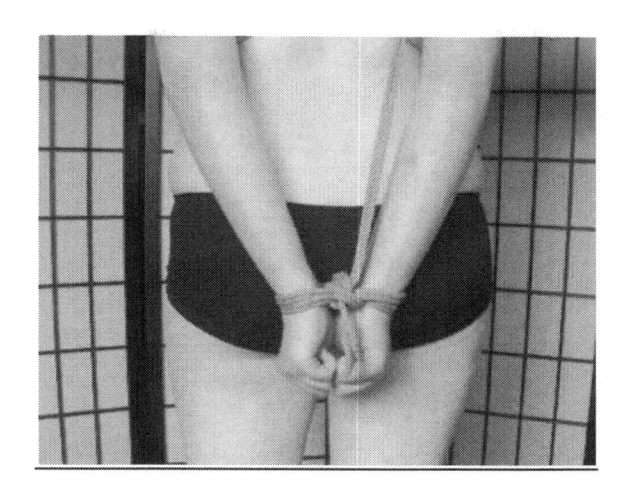

Bring the rope up until just below the elbows, then wrap around. Make sure to maintain your tension as you go. I like to put one arm around both of the rope bottom's arms to hold them together while the other hand wraps (additional dominance to the tying process, plus holds the arms together), but hey, use what works for you.

If I'm using thinner rope, then I'll wrap twice around the arms to spread the pressure, but if thicker, then once works fine.

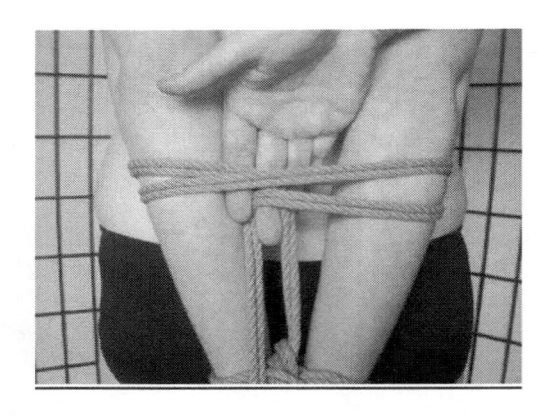

Note that I've wrapped downward; this is because I'm about to lock off tension by going back under the wraps.

So here I go creating a friction by wrapping under the bands and then pulling upward. This helps me to maintain my tension, and prevent the tie from falling apart (it does take some practice, so if you don't get it the first time, that's okay. Practice more!)

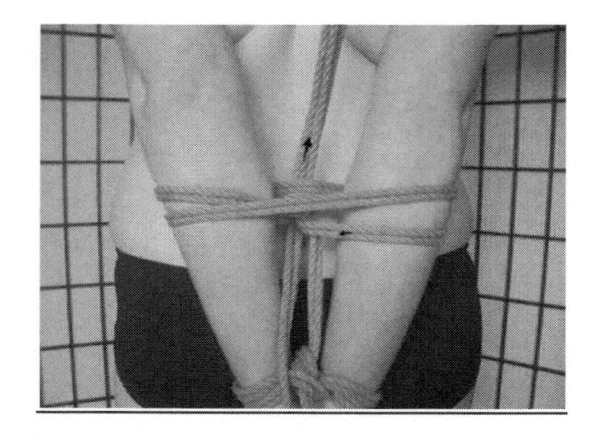

So now I've done a very simple friction by wrapping under both bands, going down again to complete the wrap, and then pulling back up. The friction has locked off my tension nicely, and looks reasonably clean and simple. (Note that this also forms a cinch; that makes it more restricting by pinching the bands behind and in front of the arms together, so they have even less room to move around.)

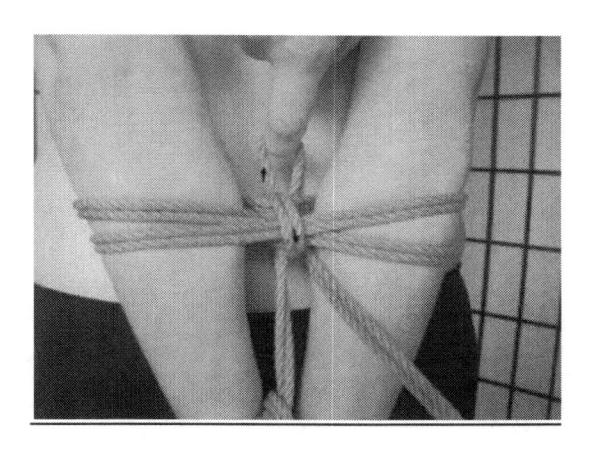

Now, I've used the exact same process to create another band above the elbows. This is because it puts less pressure on the actual joint; you do NOT want to fuck the joints up, so putting the pressure of the bands above and below the joint instead of directly on it is generally considered a wise move. In this picture below, I'm also taking a moment to dress my wraps, running my fingers below them to bunch them together. This makes certain that the tension and pressure are even, and reduces the risk of pinching skin in unpleasant ways.

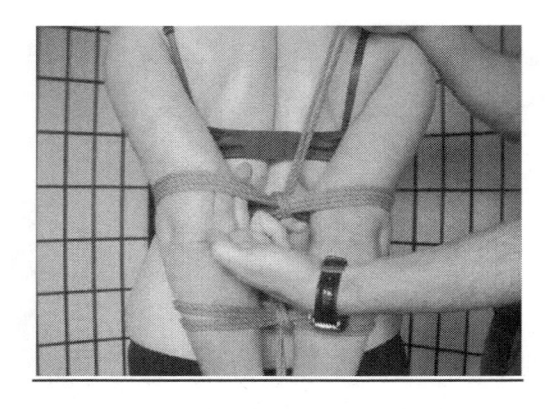

Side benefit of dressing your wraps: it makes everything look a bit prettier, neat and tidy like.

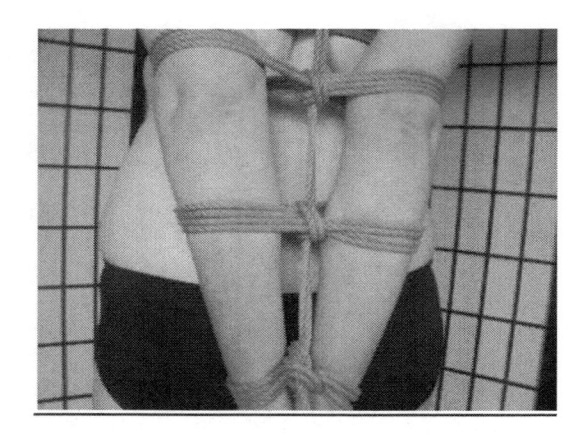

So you can put as many bands as you like on this tie; I've gone with two for simplicity's sake, but you can do more if you feel like it. Eventually though, you need to figure out some way to make the whole thing stay up. If you don't find a way to do that, the whole assembly is going to slide down the triangle that is your rope bottom's linked arms, and look silly.

I like to create a wee harness, to lock everything in place and further emphasize the breasts. Because hey. Breasts. They're pretty.

So below, I've added on some rope (slightly messily) and I'm about to create the simplest practicable harness. I could just do a couple of wraps around the chest; I have seen that done; but I like harnesses.

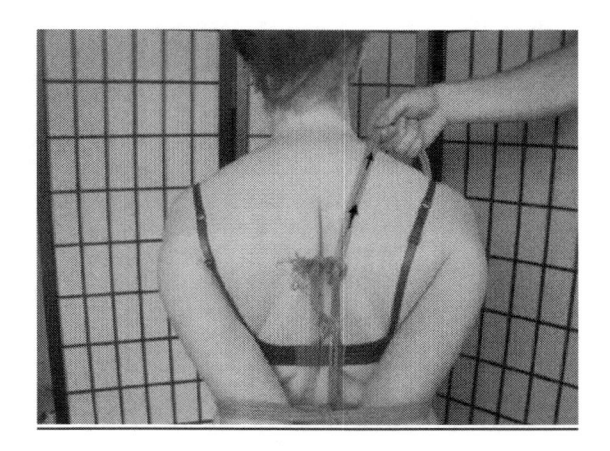

So, I bring the rope up over a shoulder, and then down on the inside of one breast.

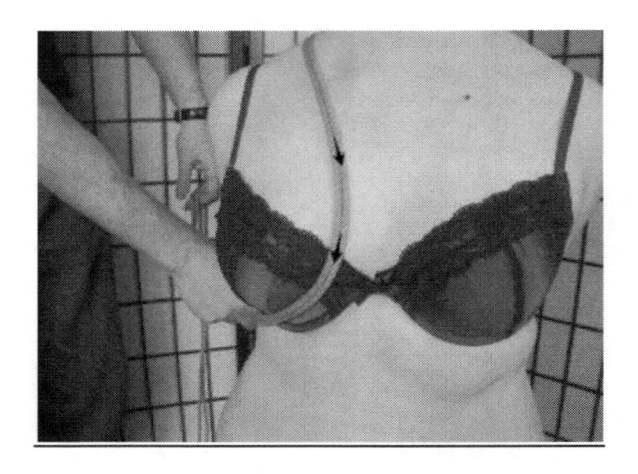

I then bring the rope down, underneath one arm, and across the back, beneath the stem of the rope going up. Going beneath looks tidier and allows the rope to lie flat against the skin.

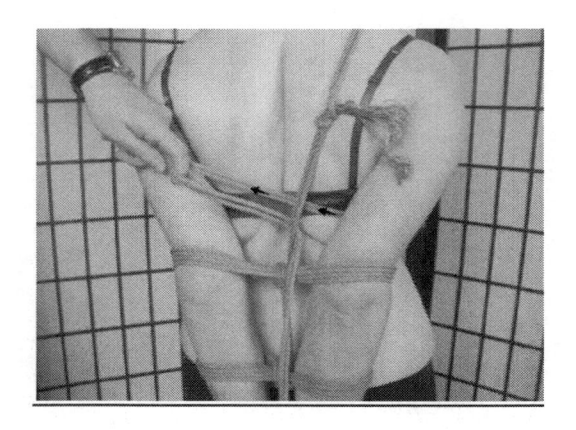

I then take the rope beneath the other arm, and up, again on the inside of the breast. I am, in effect, creating straps.

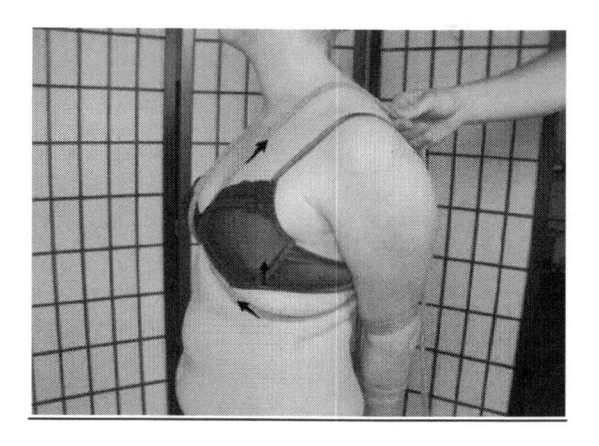

Right, now I'm bringing the rope back down to the existing intersection, and I'm about to create a neat little friction to lock off my tension before continuing.

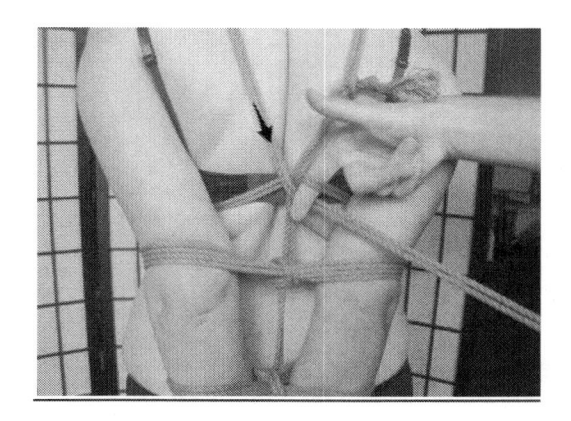

See? Very simple, but it does lock off the tension, and now allows my rope to travel horizontally.

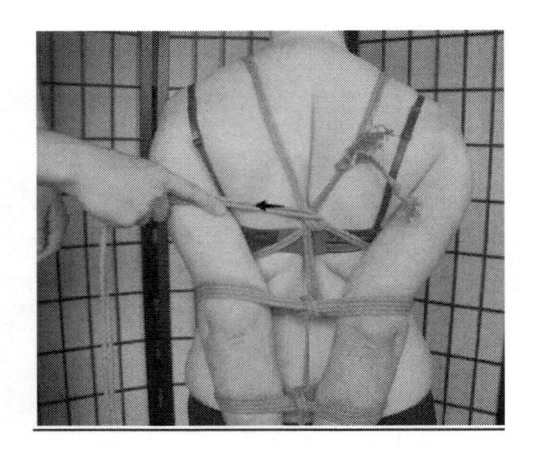

So I've brought the rope around horizontally beneath the arm, and now I'm wrapping between the two straps. This prevents them from slipping to the side and falling down the arms, which would then let the whole armbinder slide downwards.

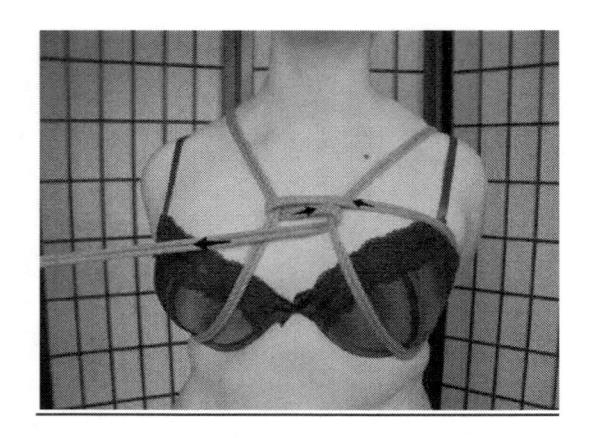

If you like, you can then vine the rope around and create a nifty little handle, but if you like the way it looks as is, there's no need. (Me, I like handles. Makes it easier to throw people around on a bed.) After the handle, I continue to bring the rope around horizontally to the back.

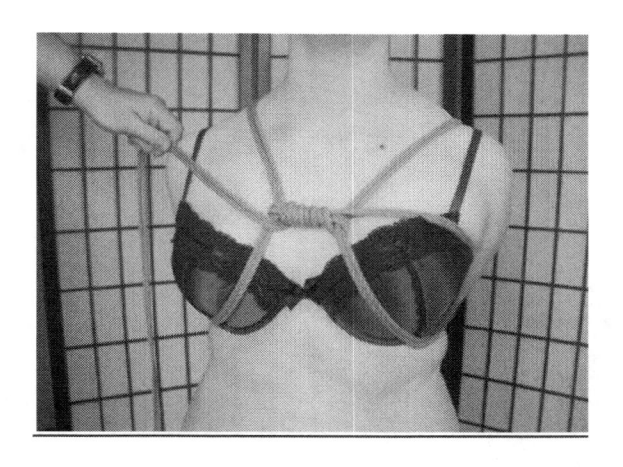

At this point, the challenge becomes deciding how to use up the rest of the rope. The harness and the arm binder tie are essentially finished; I just need to lock off. And use up all my grogram extra rope. I could get a bit artsy with it, and use my strands to separate the stem and create diamonds going downwards...

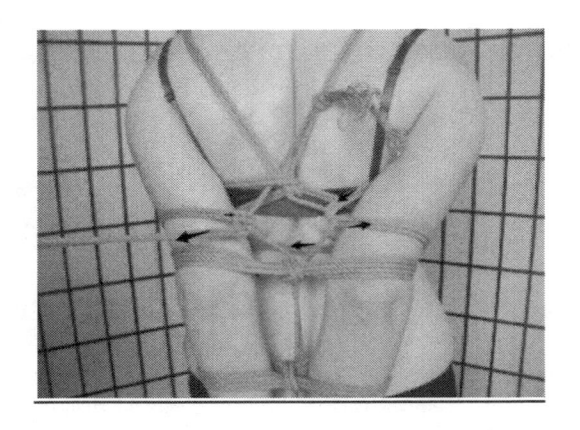

Or I could go with something a bit flatter, and vine upwards between my two rope straps. Always simple and fun to do.

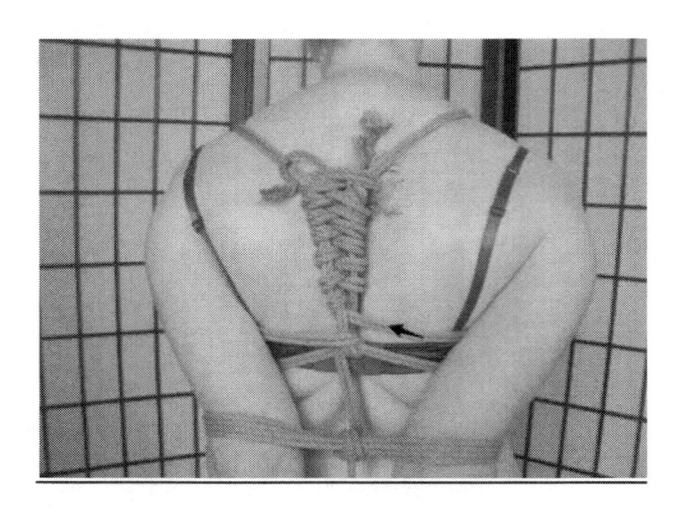

we're going to take two ties we've learned before and combine them into a hogtie. A hogtie places your bottom on the floor, face down, in either a chest harness (which we learned already) or a box tie which includes the wrists. Then, the ankles are secured to the chest ties and pulled in tightly. This tie is safer than tying the ankles to the wrists in a more Western-style hogtie as the weight of the legs is distributed across the chest instead of putting pressure on the sensitive wrists. You can either do a simple double-column tie on the ankles, or get more decorative with tying both legs into the leg tie we learned earlier.

Start by tying a chest harness on your bottom. Be sure when you extend rope for this tie that you don't have any knots right in the sternum or areas on the chest that might hurt once your bottom lies chest-down. Lay your bottom down on their belly. If you'd like to incorporate their arms, both use a new rope or the ends of the leftover rope from the chest harness and tie a single column tie around the wrists. Make sure the inside of their wrists are touching to keep the sensitive inner wrists protected. Then, tie a double column tie on their ankles.

Next, take the ends of the ankle ropes and pass them through the center column (spine) of the chest harness. Go over and do not include the ropes used to tie the wrists (if tied), so that pressure isn't being applied to the wrist tie.

Then go back and loop the rope through the bight at the ankle, and around back through the center column/spine again.

Tighten the tie until snug, but don't make sure your bottom isn't overextended and super uncomfortable. Tie off with a half hitch.

And secure with another half hitch.

If you find the rope places too much pressure on the wrists, you can try tying it around the top of the chest harness instead. Pass the ropes behind both shoulder ropes, right above the top knot, and tie off the same way.

You'll need a new rope to knot a single column tie around both ankle ropes to the chest harness if you want to be more aesthetically pleasing and use leg ties rather than the double column tie. Using the same pulley technique as the tie above, attach that new rope to the chest harness. To avoid tying the legs together, you can even use two different ropes to bind the ankles apart.

How To Tie A Chest Harness

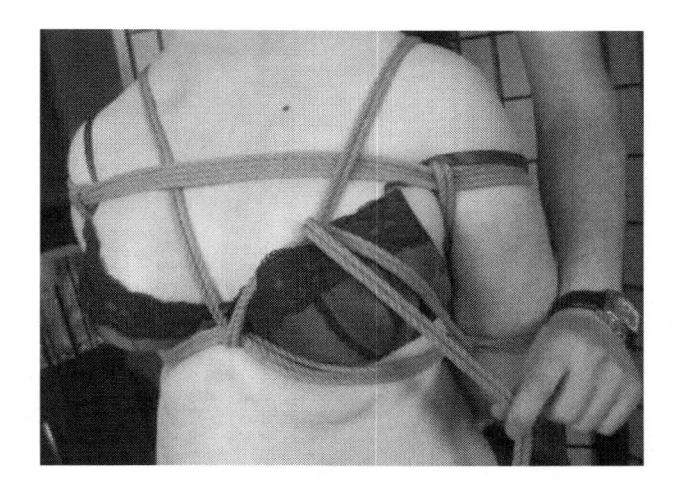

For this post, I'm going to be going over the basic principles of tying a chest harness, which is a pretty awesome tie. I use them a LOT, for various different purposes.

- The post will cover
- what they're used for

- limitations of the harness

- and the important principles of how to tie them.

- What I Would Use It For

Chest harnesses are actually good for a lot of different things.

Use The First:

Shibari style chest harnesses are decorative as all hell. The first time I saw one in person I was at a party, and I watched in awe as this scantily clad chick wandered past me, smiling slightly, looking mysterious as all hell in this apparently intricate, decorative piece of foreign bondage.

And of course, they emphasize the chest. Enough said.

They're freaking GREAT for photos.

Use The Second:

Properly tied, a chest harness is actually restrictive. Individual bottoms may have more or less trouble wiggling out of it; I find that people with shorter arms tend to find it easier to escape these. However, tied snugly and well cinched, people will find them quite restrictive and not that easy to get out of.

A good chest harness is also effective for making someone feel helpless and really emphasizing that sense of being bound; with all that rope crossing the chest and other places, you really feel caught up in rope. As a guy, it's an interesting feeling trying to flex against all that restriction; there's a definite sense of the usual masculine power (upper body strength) being locked down.

Use The Third:

A chest harness makes for a really solid anchoring point. You can tie other things to it really easily, and all that rope spreads the load or pressure across the torso instead of concentrating it in any one place. As an example, if you couldn't do a chest harness beginning with the arms, then you can do one beginning with a single column tie around the torso and then attach the arms to it somewhere later on.

This same principle of spreading the load and making a good anchoring point also makes chest harnesses very useful for partial or full suspension of the body's weight off the ground. That's risky business, with increased risk; but it's still a lot of fun, particularly partial suspensions.

I've also used chest harnesses in the past with a safety line to keep someone standing without fear of falling down. Useful when you have someone standing blindfolded and you can't put strain on their wrists due to a previous injury – the harness makes for a much safer anchor point than tying their wrists above their head, for example.

Note: The chest harness shown below is a "floor play" harness. In order to make it better for suspension, there are a number of refinements that would need to be added for that, as discussed at the bottom of the post.

Use the Fourth:

If you're one of those people that uses rope as a means of interactions instead of just using it for restriction - by which I mean you do connective bondage— then chest harnesses are for you. They take a decent length of time to tie, during which you have LOTS of opportunity to interact with whoever you're tying. Sliding the rope in a caressing motion across the skin, yanking a friction closed with a forceful movement, forcing your rope bottom's body to move according to your will as you tie them... it makes for a lot of fun. And by the time you finish the tie, the person in your rope has already been very, very affected by the tying process, and they're already well into that "play" headspace.

Limitations:

Rope bottoms with limited flexibility may have trouble keeping their hands/arms behind their back in order to do the style of chest harness depicted here.

Because of the placement of the bands over the arms, care must be taken to ensure that the radial nerve doesn't have a lot of pressure placed on it.

How To Create The Chest Harness

The basic principles of chest harnesses go like this:

Start off with a single column tie – usually around the wrists behind the back, but sometimes on the torso.

Moving upward, create wraps or bands going around the whole torso, usually including the arms.

Use frictions to lock your wraps/bands in place against the stem

Use cinches between torso and arms to make the whole thing more restrictive and stop your wraps from going up over the shoulders.

Find a decorative way to finish and tie off.

Here's how to do it in pictures

Start with the single column tie around both wrists. Refer to – as you'll see, most ties start off with a single column tie. Try and make sure your bottom has the inside of the wrists facing each other; it's a lot safer in terms of circulation, tendons, etc.

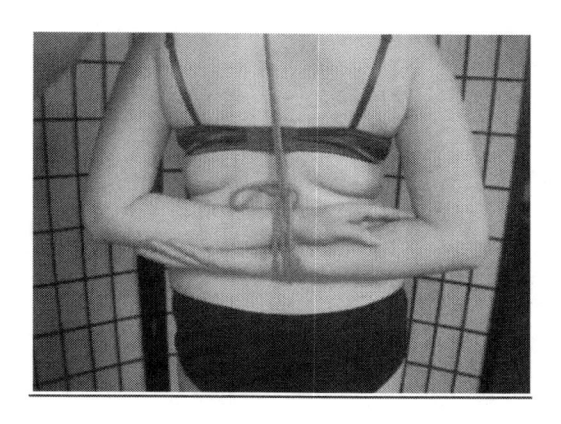

Bring the rope up the back; you want it a few inches below the top of the arms. Then take it at right angles around to the front of the body.

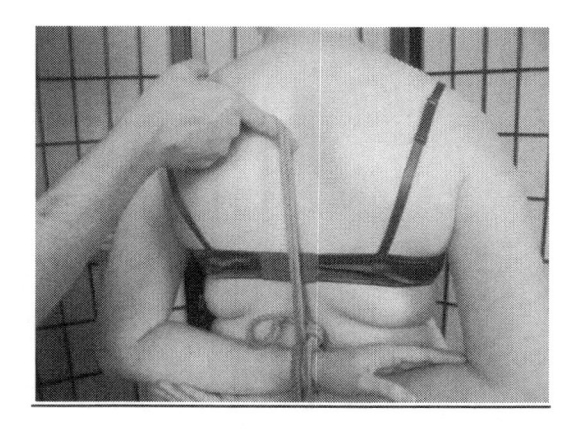

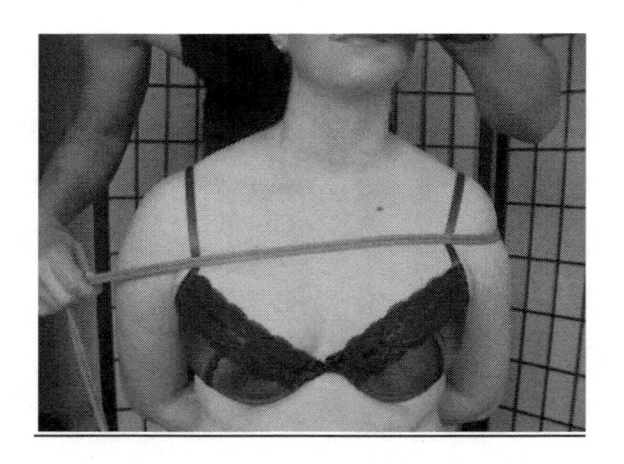

Bringing the rope back around to the back, I'm going around the stem, and then reversing and going back the way I came. That's a personal preference; some encourage keeping on going around to create the second wrap, but I find that this is more convenient for maintaining my tension and holding everything in place.

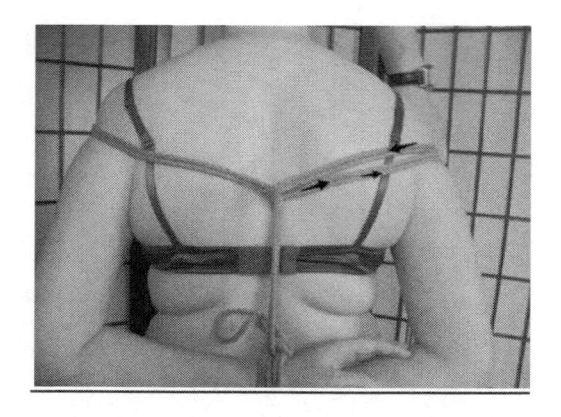

I now go back around the front to make my band of rope a bit thicker; as with any tie, the more wraps, the thicker the band, and the more comfortable and supportive it is.

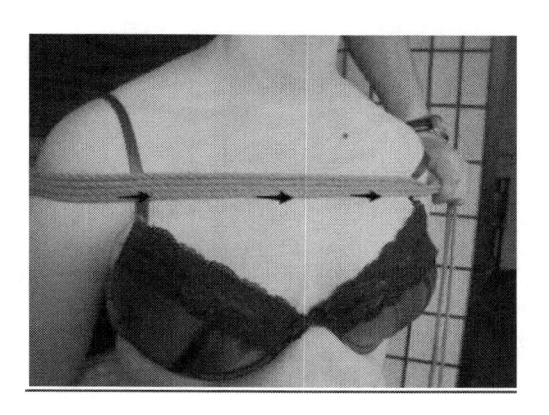

Okay, made it to the back; now I've again wrapped around my stem to balance out my tension, and I'm about to form my first friction. Frictions are great; they hold everything in place while still being easy to undo later.

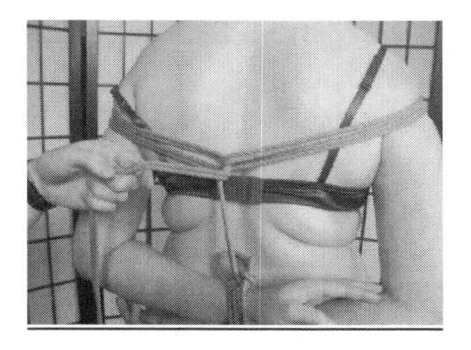

Working end goes in front of the stem, then under the band.

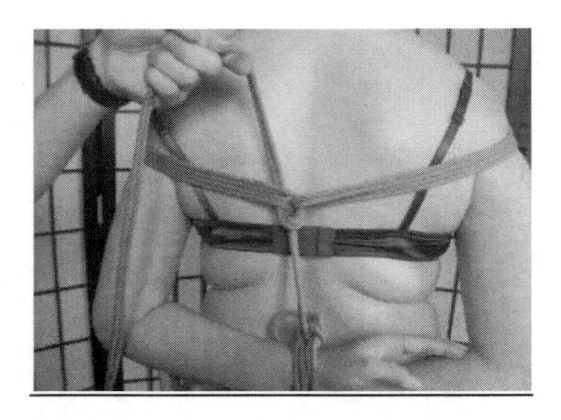

Working end is pulled down to one side.

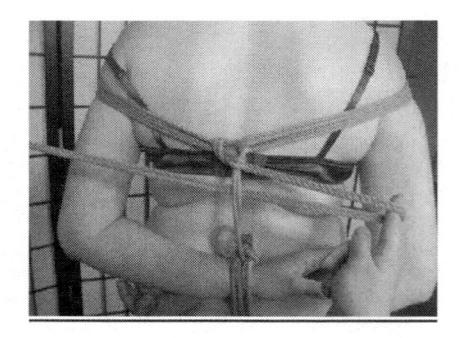

Then up and over the stem again, coming down behind it.

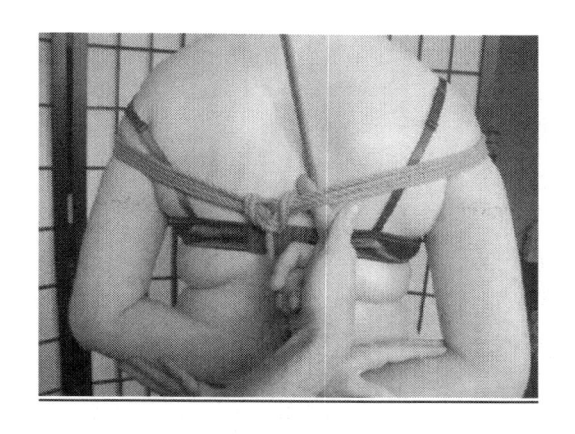

And finally wrapping horizontally around the stem again to balance the tension before going to one side. Note: This is not the only way to do a friction, but it's probably my favorite due to the symmetry. Anything that locks off your tension and lets you take the rope in the correct direction will work. These frictions are firm, but not as tight as they could be; for supporting load you want to compact them down tighter. I'm now about to create my first cinch.

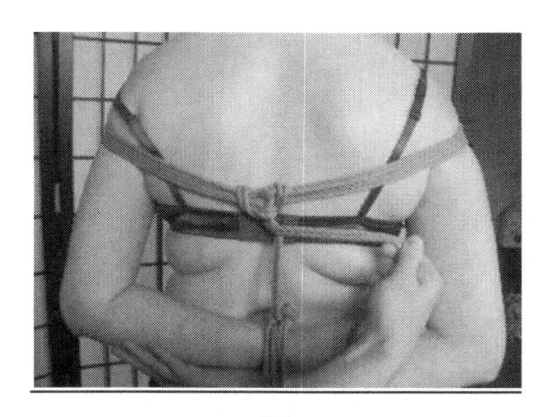

This is my first cinch. I've taken the rope that went to the side up between the arm and the chest, and carefully pulled it beneath the band of rope, and then pulled it downward over the band again. This is to lock the band in place and prevent it from sliding up over the shoulder. Sliding a thumb under the band has helped me create the gap that let me pull the rope through with minimal discomfort to the lovely lady here.

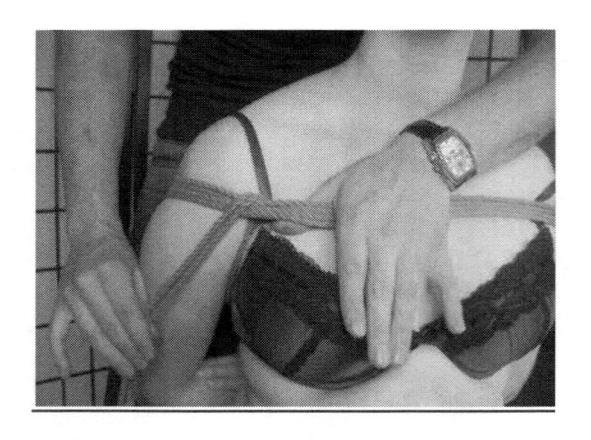

I've brought the rope back through the gap between arm and torso, and under the stem (to keep it reasonably neat) as I move back around to the other side to make my second cinch. You'll note that I've added rope as I wrapped across the back; refer to How To Join Your Rope for instructions on this.

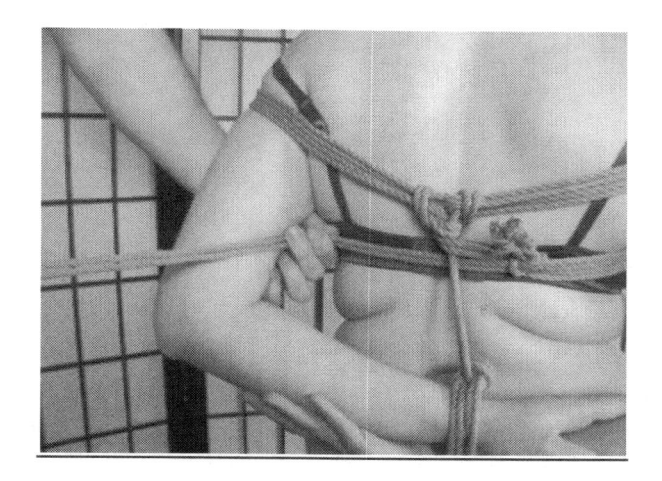

As you can see, the second cinch is exactly the same as the first.

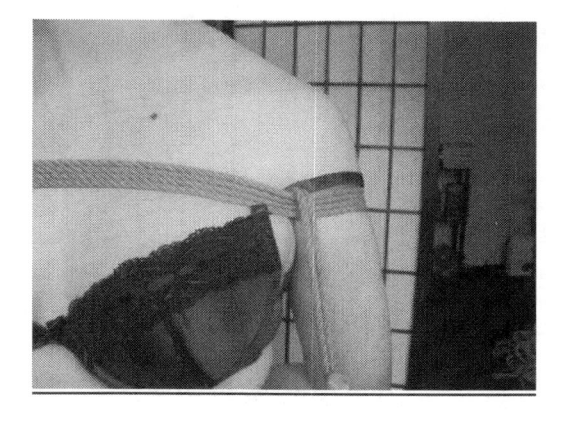

Okay, so now I've wrapped the cinch around the stem, and now I'm about to make my second band across the lower part of the arms.

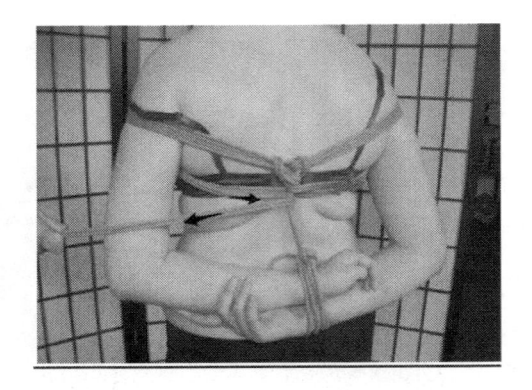

Around the front again, below the breasts.

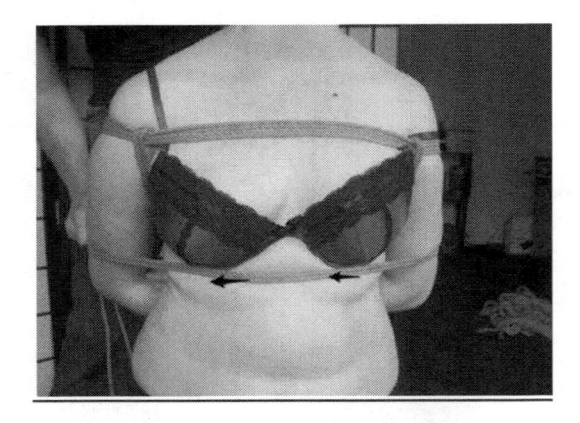

And then again using the stem to maintain tension as I go back. Yes, it is distorting my stem somewhat; that's not a serious issue, and it can be fixed by adjusting the tension as I finish up these wraps.

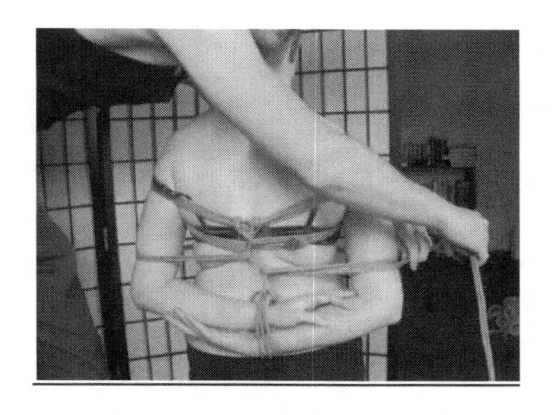

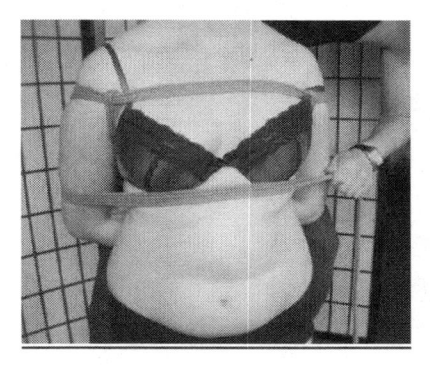

The process for making the second friction is exactly the same as the first. This is me halfway through it; yes, it will take practice. It looks nice when you're done, though, and sits reasonably flat against the back.

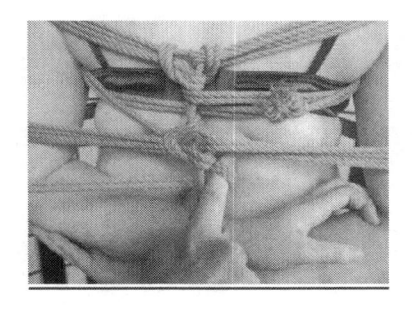

Again, once the friction is done, it's time to cinch the band. Exactly the same process as the first time. These cinches add more restriction to the tie, giving the arms less room to wiggle around.

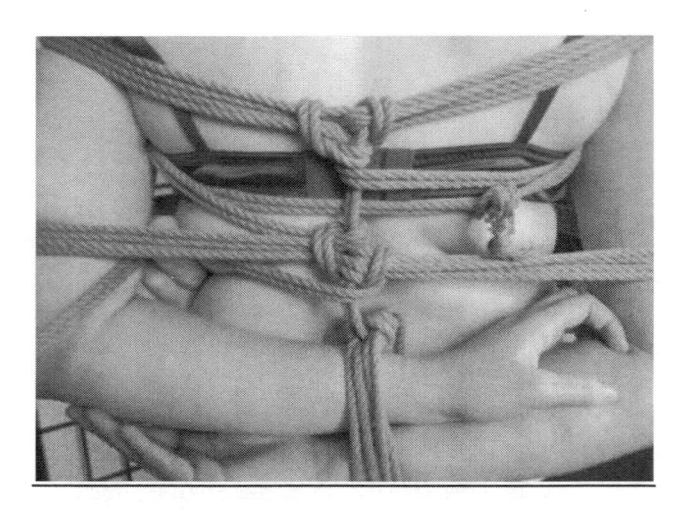

Same process as the top one, then back across the back beneath the stem to do your other one.

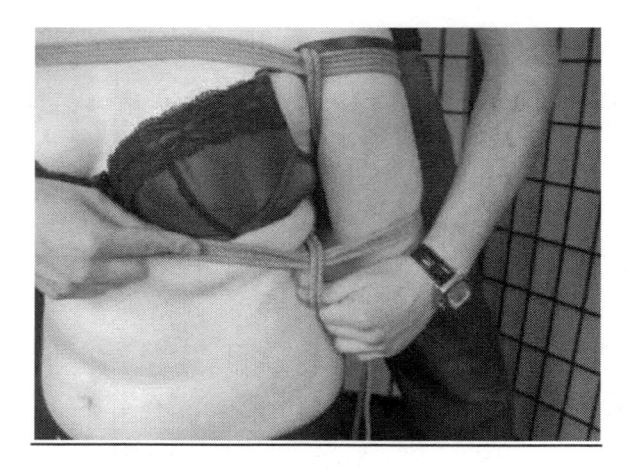

For all intents and purposes, we now have a functional (non-suspension) play or decorative harness. We have two solid bands, which provide good restriction. We have top cinches which prevent the top band for slipping off over the shoulders, and bottom cinches to restrict the movement of the arms. We're good. All we really need to do is tie off somehow; a slip-knot or veining or using a Cow-Hitch (refer to 3 Ways To Improve The Look Of Your Bondage) and we're done.

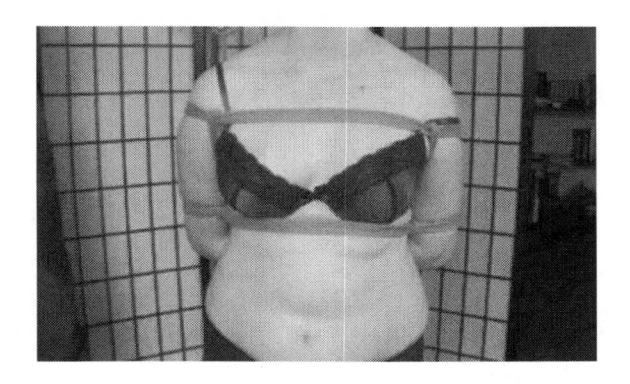

But then we miss an opportunity to make something pretty.

Here, I've brought my last cinch back around, wrapped around the base of the stem, and brought it up at an angle. I've used a Munter Hitch (3 Ways To Improve The Look Of Your Bondage) to secure the rope to the top band (could have just used a twist, but I'm a fussy fancy pants) and now I'm bringing it up over the shoulder.

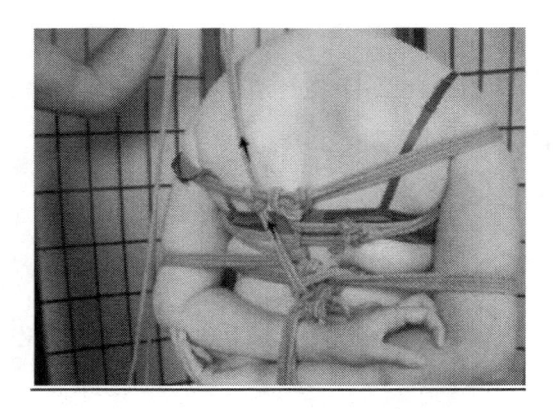

I've brought the rope down over the shoulder, and bent it around the bottom wrap between the breasts, creating a V. Because hey, breasts. And I suppose it keeps the bottom band in place, too... but really it's just fun to emphasize breasts and chests further.

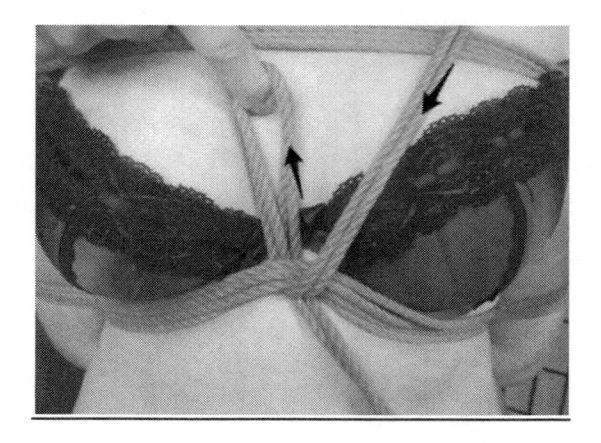

Having created my V, I've now brought the rope back over and then down the other shoulder. I've created another hitch for symmetry. Again, I could easily lock off here to finish the tie, but there's a neat trick that makes V shape harnesses more comfortable, preventing them from digging into the neck.

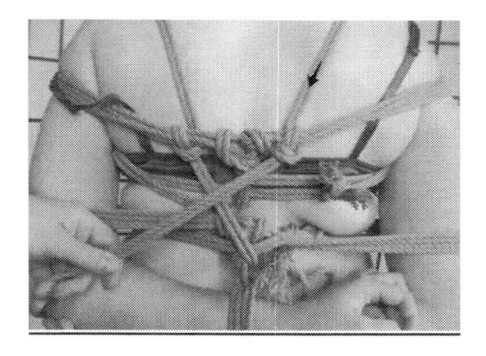

Taking the rope back beneath the arm, I'm about to create a sort of cinch.

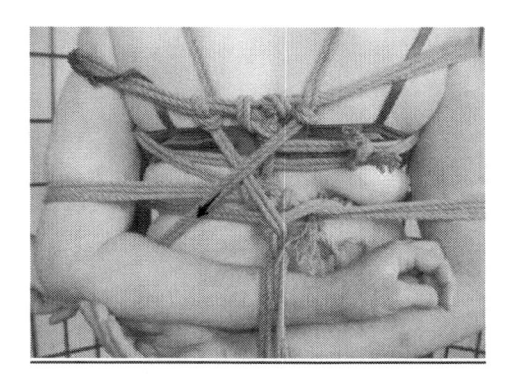

By pulling the sides of the V away at a slight angle, I reduce the risk of the V digging into the neck. You don't have to pull it far. You then run the rope behind the back, behind the stem again, and do the same on the other side.

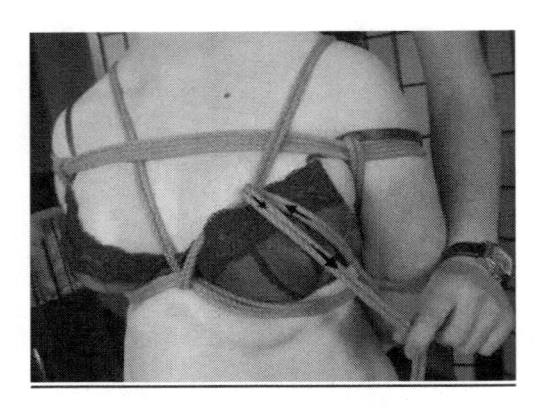

Here's the other side done.

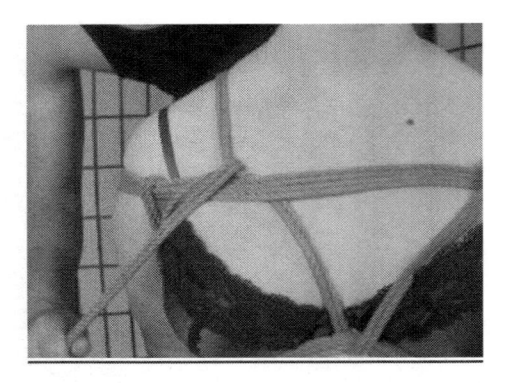

Now, I actually forgot to get a picture of the finished tie from this side. It was a busy afternoon, all right? So

I just invited a friend around to recreate the tie and make sure you all got a decent view of the finished pattern. In fact, you get two, because I'm feeling nice.

Pretty, right? And really practical and comfortable. I really enjoy chest harnesses. For practical as well as obvious reasons.

Finishing at the back isn't hard. You can bring the rope up to the stem and tie off using a similar method as the third one in Tying People To Things. It's basically a slip knot, which is safe, because it's tied only to rope.

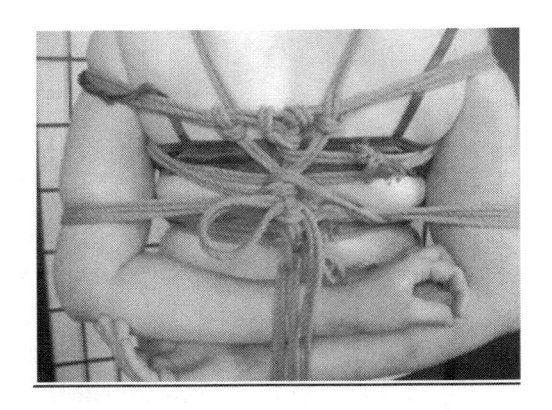

Or you can do a similar thing as in **How To Tie A Rope Armbinder**, where you take the rope upwards and vine between straps.

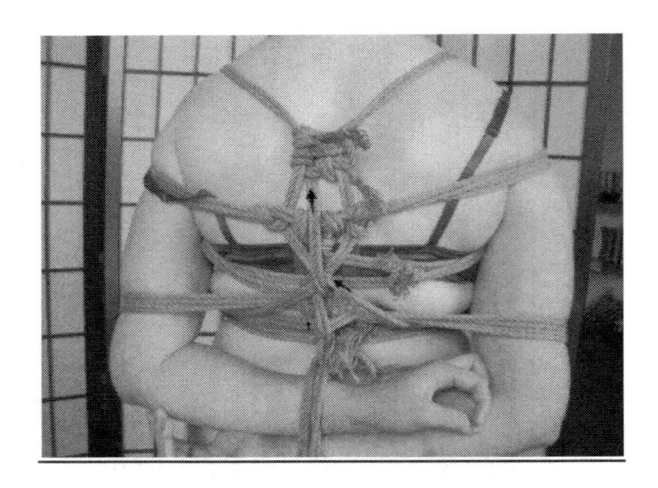

When I was first starting out with rope, I had trouble understanding the appeal of it. I certainly had no idea of how popular it was, the doors it could open, and the many benefits it could add to my life.

Which, by the way, were significant.

And I think the reason why I was so in the dark, was because nobody in mainstream society really talks about it. They might mention that someone "likes being tied up" and nod and wink and chuckle about it, but they don't tend to go into further detail. It's left a mystery.

This is freaking frustrating for people who want to know more about it!

It can be difficult for people to understand the appeal of rope without someone actually taking the time to point the way, to give them a starting point. I know it took me a long time, because nobody actually went to the trouble to articulate it. They expected me to somehow mysteriously know. And when I didn't know, it felt like that old childish thing, "If you don't know, I'm not going to tell you."

Which is probably a little unfair – maybe they didn't know how to say it. But that's how it felt.

I don't want that for other people. So I'm going into endless amounts of detail on the "why", and the "what" as well as the "how".

This is information that is probably most useful for when you're starting out; but it's information that I wish I'd had back at the beginning of my journey. So I've put together a brief list of some of the benefits that come to my mind when I think about the fun and joy of playing with rope.

A note: different people find different benefits and different things to enjoy in rope. I wouldn't expect everyone to appreciate all the things about rope; but if there's something in this post that ignites a spark, something that really appeals, then I'd say there's a very high likelihood that rope bondage is for you.

Chapter Six

The Benefits

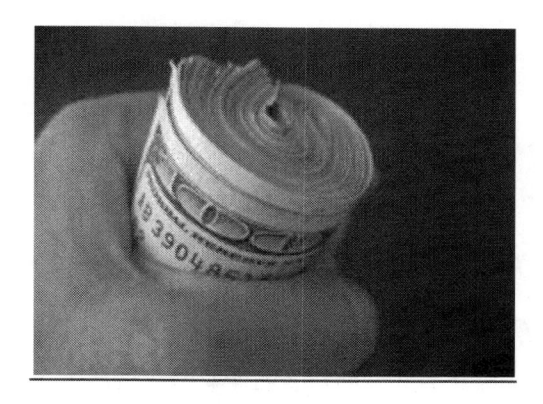

Get the best value

Versatility/Cost Effective Toys

For couples exploring bondage, rope is one of the most versatile, cost effective means of restraint available. BDSM toys can be EXPENSIVE. Rather than spending hundreds of dollars on expensive leather cuffs (that can only restrain in a couple of ways) and a high priced flogger, couples who invest in a few lengths of rope for less than the price of the cuffs can create an almost infinite variety of restraints; they can also create blindfolds, gags, impact toys (including floggers), and anything else their imaginations can conjure. And once they're done with one thing, they can untie it and use it for something else, before storing their rope neatly in a drawer.

DemonstrableSKILL

the benefits are similar for a new dominant; however, not only does the new dominant have a VERY affordable set of restraints and toys in his or her few lengths of rope, they also have a clearly demonstrable skill, one that's taken time and patience to learn. That is freaking GOLD when exploring the possibilities of connection or play with a submissive; because any self respecting submissive will be looking for something to respect in a prospective dominant. Demonstrating patience, appreciation of safety, skill and confidence with your rope will definitely get you started on that. It's also a great way to create friendships and earn respect in the BDSM community; building your skill, demonstrating it responsibly, and sharing it (without being an arrogant prick) will go a long way with others.

Extra Satisfaction

For the rope top, there are multiple levels of satisfaction in working with rope. You get to master the rope; learning its intricacies, how it moves, how to control it; and then you get to use that mastery and knowledge to affect and control another person. Effectively dominating both your rope and the person tied in your rope. There's something very appealing about that idea...

Decoration

When you tie a person up, you can make them look freaking HOT. There are so many decorative ways to tie someone, but some examples; corset harnesses, "damsel in distress" ties, spider webs, any number of intricate and appealing ties. (This is why rope bondage photos are so damn popular on Fetlife). You can tie a person in such a way as to provocatively show off their assets "against their will", and you can use it to accentuate, accessorize, and highlight just how hot a person is; and why you want to ravish them so badly

I don't know about you, but I love making a person feel sexy; And it's definitely fun showing off the combination of their sexiness with my rope work.

You would be amazed at the doors these skills can open for you... and what it can lead Opportunities For Relationships. Skills with rope bondage can open doorways and bring you relationships you might not otherwise have. Fun fact; there is a very significant percentage of the population who wonder, are curious about, or who actively fantasize about being tied up. Another fun fact: compared to the general population, there aren't really that many people skilled with rope around...Therefore, people with rope skills gain significant value and attraction points to this percentage, and are in high demand. It's always nice to have a few extra selling points and opportunities – as well as new and different ways to connect with people.

Exploring Connection and Intensity. Rope does not create connection (people do) but holy hell does it facilitate it when applied appropriately. How you tie a person, the interaction between your feelings and theirs, the way they become focused on you and your movements, and your awareness of them in your rope... it's something that has to be experienced to truly be understood or appreciated. It's intense. It can deepen and intensify relationships like you would not believe; through trust, through shared experience, through closeness and intimacy. Some people tie others without ever having it turn sexual; because they don't need it to. The closeness, the intimacy, the connection; that's what they get out of it.

Helping People Become Art Rope bondage and photography can transform a person from being their everyday selves to being an amazing piece of art. That's a very empowering thing for some, especially those who really love the immortality or expressionism of art. Others find it a wonderfully transformative experience which allows them to see and experience their own beauty in new ways.

Creating Art (with or without tying someone up) When you develop skill at tying, you can apply it to different arenas. Rope can provide an unusual means of interacting with your environment. It is possible to create some amazing art with no human models at all; but rather through using rope to bind objects, control space, and effect symbolic meanings or representations through suggesting at certain shapes. Color of rope, environment, objects, types and style of tying; all of it plays a part in your finished piece.

Rough Play/Capture Sometimes rope bondage is about the struggle; being caught, overpowered, tied mean and hard and rough, until finally the person in rope has to give in, to admit defeat. That can be what arouses ; being overpowered, mastered, captured by someone else's skill and strength, having them "earn" the right to do as they want with the tied up person's body. There can be S&M elements involved; trust me, it is not difficult at all for a rope top to provide harsher sensations for those that enjoy them. Other times it's more about the enjoyment of (consensual and negotiated) fantasies of non-consent. This can be pretty fun, when properly negotiated/discussed first.

Submission/Freedom

Other times rope bondage creates an opportunity for a person in rope to submit to the whim of the other; the ties, the positions, the speed and mood, all decided upon and made to happen by the person tying. They can find it incredibly freeing; suddenly there's no performance anxiety at all, because the other person makes all the decisions. Some people have even found themselves able to orgasm in bondage when they never, ever could before. Others have just gotten a massive happy from obeying or submitting. Being a human canvas for art, or a subject for "science" (creating new ties, testing new knots, etc) can be immensely satisfying for the submissively inclined. It may have nothing to do with play; and everything to do with serving, being useful, or making someone else happy. I personally haven't had that experience, but I am assured by submissive I know that this is so.

THANK YOU

Made in the USA
Las Vegas, NV
02 September 2023